Learning PyTorch 2.0

Experiment deep learning from basics to complex models using every potential capability of Pythonic PyTorch

Matthew Rosch

Published by: GitforGits
Publisher: Sonal Dhandre
www.gitforgits.com
support@gitforgits.com

Printed in India

First Printing: July 2023

ISBN: 978-8196288372

Cover Design by: Kitten Publishing

For permission to use material from this book, please contact GitforGits at support@gitforgits.com.

Prologue

Dear reader, we are excited to take you on an exciting adventure into the fascinating world of PyTorch 2.0. This book has been painstakingly developed as a thorough reference, with the intention of illuminating the complex terrain of deep learning. Its goal is to change you from a curious enthusiast into a proficient practitioner by providing you with the theoretical understanding as well as the practical expertise necessary to properly use PyTorch. While we embark on this journey of discovery, we want you to participate completely by testing the validity of your previously held beliefs and broadening your perspective on the fascinating field of deep learning.

The first part of the book lays a strong basis in the fundamental principles that underpin PyTorch. Tensors, the fundamental building elements of PyTorch, are the subject of substantial discussion in the first few chapters. These first few chapters will walk you through the steps of comprehending tensors, as well as the process of building and manipulating them. This book will ensure that you have a solid foundation in the fundamentals before going on to more advanced ideas by gradually increasing the difficulty of the topics as you progress through it.

As we continue to delve further into the workings of PyTorch, the book begins to introduce the development of basic as well as more complex models. We break down the many parts that make up these models with the help of some examples to illustrate our points. You will gain knowledge on how to create and train a variety of neural networks, including feed-forward and recurrent neural networks, as well as GRUs and CNNs, which are more advanced models. You will be able to apply what you learn in the book to real-world situations since it combines theoretical explanations with real-world examples, which helps to drive home the many concepts and methods that are covered.

The knowledge of the training process comes next in the book, after an initial look at neural networks. Unraveling optimization algorithms, sometimes known as the "engines that drive learning in neural networks," is one of the most important aspects of this endeavor. The book explains each algorithm in a manner that is both comprehensive and easy to understand, beginning with the fundamental Gradient Descent and progressing all the way up to the more complex Adaptive Moment Estimation. You will now have the ability to construct and train robust models using PyTorch thanks to the knowledge and the activities you have completed.

In the latter chapters of this book, we delve into the more sophisticated principles of the PyTorch programming language. You will acquire knowledge regarding the serialization and optimization of models, as well as the use of distributed training and the Quantization API provided by PyTorch. In addition, we investigate the connection between TensorFlow 2.0 and PyTorch 2.0, comparing and contrasting the advantages and disadvantages of both programs. In doing so, the book arms you with the knowledge necessary to select the framework that caters to your requirements in the most optimal manner.

As we embark on this adventure, we want to urge you to approach each chapter with an open heart and a mind that is full of curiosity. This book offers something to offer everyone, from someone who is just beginning out in deep learning to someone who is an experienced professional looking to develop their skills. We have high hopes that by the time you finish reading this book, you will not only have a comprehensive understanding of PyTorch 2.0 but also the self-assurance to put what you have learned into practice in the real world. Let's not waste any more time and go right into this thrilling adventure together, shall we? PyTorch 2.0 is where you want to be, so welcome!

Content

Preface

This book is a comprehensive guide to understanding and utilizing PyTorch 2.0 for deep learning applications. It starts with an introduction to PyTorch, its various advantages over other deep learning frameworks, and its blend with CUDA for GPU acceleration. We delve into the heart of PyTorch – tensors, learning their different types, properties, and operations. Through step-by-step examples, the reader learns to perform basic arithmetic operations on tensors, manipulate them, and understand errors related to tensor shapes.

A substantial portion of the book is dedicated to illustrating how to build simple PyTorch models. This includes uploading and preparing datasets, defining the architecture, training, and predicting. It provides hands-on exercises with a real-world dataset. The book then segues into exploring PyTorch's nn module and gives a detailed comparison of different types of networks like Feedforward, RNN, GRU, CNN, and their combination.

Further, the book delves into understanding the training process and PyTorch's optim module. It explores the overview of optimization algorithms like Gradient Descent, SGD, Mini-batch Gradient Descent, Momentum, Adagrad, and Adam. A separate chapter focuses on advanced concepts in PyTorch 2.0, like model serialization, optimization, distributed training, and PyTorch Quantization API.

In the final chapters, the book discusses the differences between TensorFlow 2.0 and PyTorch 2.0 and the step-by-step process of migrating a TensorFlow model to PyTorch 2.0 using ONNX. It provides an overview of common issues encountered during this process and how to resolve them.

In this book you will learn:

- A comprehensive introduction to PyTorch and CUDA for deep learning.
- Detailed understanding and operations on PyTorch tensors.
- Step-by-step guide to building simple PyTorch models.
- Insight into PyTorch's nn module and comparison of various network types.
- Overview of the training process and exploration of PyTorch's optim module.
- Understanding advanced concepts in PyTorch like model serialization and optimization.
- Knowledge on distributed training in PyTorch.
- Practical guide to using PyTorch's Quantization API.
- Differences between TensorFlow 2.0 and PyTorch 2.0.

- Guidance on migrating TensorFlow models to PyTorch using ONNX.

The book equips the reader with comprehensive knowledge of PyTorch 2.0 and provides practical examples to apply this knowledge, making it an ideal read for aspiring network administrators.

GitforGits

Prerequisites

A perfect and skillful book for every machine learning engineer, data scientist, AI engineer and data researchers who are passionately looking towards drawing actionable intelligence using PyTorch 2.0. Knowing Python and basics of deep learning is all you need to sail through this book.

Codes Usage

Are you in need of some helpful code examples to assist you in your programming and documentation? Look no further! Our book offers a wealth of supplemental material, including code examples and exercises.

Not only is this book here to aid you in getting your job done, but you have our permission to use the example code in your programs and documentation. However, please note that if you are reproducing a significant portion of the code, we do require you to contact us for permission.

But don't worry, using several chunks of code from this book in your program or answering a question by citing our book and quoting example code does not require permission. But if you do choose to give credit, an attribution typically includes the title, author, publisher, and ISBN. For example, "Learning PyTorch 2.0 by Matthew Rosch".

If you are unsure whether your intended use of the code examples falls under fair use or the permissions outlined above, please do not hesitate to reach out to us at support@gitforgits.com.

We are happy to assist and clarify any concerns.

Acknowledgement

I owe a tremendous debt of gratitude to GitforGits, for their unflagging enthusiasm and wise counsel throughout the entire process of writing this book. Their knowledge and careful editing helped make sure the piece was useful for people of all reading levels and comprehension skills. In addition, I'd like to thank everyone involved in the publishing process for their efforts in making this book a reality. Their efforts, from copyediting to advertising, made the project what it is today.

Finally, I'd like to express my gratitude to everyone who has shown me unconditional love and encouragement throughout my life. Their support was crucial to the completion of this book. I appreciate your help with this endeavour and your continued interest in my career.

Chapter 1: Introduction To PyTorch 2.0 and CUDA 11.8

Essentials of Neural Networks

An fascinating computer model known as the artificial neural network captures the essence of deep learning, a subset of machine learning. Deep learning is a subset of machine learning. In this chapter, we investigate the fundamentals of neural networks, including their applicability to deep learning and the manner in which these models imitate the fundamental processes carried out by the human brain.

Artificial neurons make up the processing units that make up neural networks, which are collections of interconnected nodes. These networks take their design cues from real neurons, which are the essential building blocks of the brain. Artificial neurons and the connections between them form the basis for the intellectual capabilities of deep learning systems. Just as billions of neurons connected by synapses allow people to learn, see, and react to the environment around them, so do artificial neurons and their connections.

Anatomy of a Neural Network

Artificial neural networks are typically structured in layers, starting with an input layer, one or more hidden layers, and an output layer. Each layer consists of multiple artificial neurons, also known as nodes.

- Input Layer: The input layer is responsible for receiving raw data from the outside world. This data is then fed into the network to be processed. Each node in this layer represents a single feature from the input dataset.

- Hidden Layers: The hidden layers are where the actual processing is done via a system of connections characterized by weights and biases. These layers transform the input into something the output layer can use.

- Output Layer: The output layer is responsible for producing the final result or decision. The number of nodes in the output layer is often determined by the nature of the problem - for instance, a binary classification problem would have one node, while a multi-class problem would have nodes equivalent to the number of classes.

Each node is interconnected with nodes of the preceding and succeeding layers. These connections are associated with weights, which dictate the importance or influence of a particular input. Furthermore, each node has a bias that allows the activation function's threshold to be shifted.

Learning in a Neural Network

Given a collection of input-output pairs, the process of "learning" in neural networks is making adjustments to these weights and biases in accordance with the error that the network generates. A loss function is used to calculate this error. A loss function is a function that measures the difference between the prediction made by the network and the actual output.

Backpropagation is the process of updating the weights and biases of a network by sending an error signal back through the network and then propagating that error. When trying to identify the ideal collection of weights and biases that will result in the smallest possible loss function, optimization procedures such as gradient descent are utilized.

Neural Network and Deep Learning

Neural networks form the backbone of deep learning. A 'deep' neural network simply refers to a network with multiple hidden layers. These deeper networks are capable of capturing complex patterns and representations in the input data, making them incredibly powerful tools for tasks like image recognition, natural language processing, and more.

However, training deep neural networks is a non-trivial task. As we add more layers, we increase the model's complexity and thus the computational burden. Thankfully, advances in hardware (GPUs), along with efficient software platforms like PyTorch, have made the training of deep networks feasible and more accessible.

In the upcoming chapters, we will delve deeper into PyTorch and how it can be leveraged to build and train neural networks. We will also explore how it has been optimized for GPU acceleration, using CUDA 11.8, significantly speeding up the process of training deep neural networks. In essence, neural networks, by emulating the structure and functionality of the human brain, have revolutionized the field of artificial intelligence. They have opened new avenues for developing intelligent systems capable of performing complex tasks with little to no explicit programming, thus marking the dawn of an exciting era in technology.

Introduction to PyTorch

Now that we are familiar with the fundamentals of neural networks, we will move on to discuss PyTorch, a tool that plays a vital role in the process of developing and training these networks.

PyTorch Overview

Developed by the Facebook AI Research lab (FAIR), PyTorch is a powerful, open-source deep learning framework that provides the flexibility and speed necessary for scientific computing. Known for its dynamic computational graph and user-friendly interface, PyTorch has quickly become the tool of choice for researchers and developers in the AI field.

How PyTorch supports Deep Learning

PyTorch is famous for its define-by-run methodology, which means that it enables dynamic computational graphs. This is one of the reasons why PyTorch is so popular. PyTorch is ideally suited for simulations that call for intricate control flow components such as loops and conditionals because of its flexibility, which enables the development and updating of systems in a comprehensible manner as calculations are being carried out.

PyTorch's application programming interface (API) is intended to be user-friendly and simple to explore. PyTorch is able to enable developers to use native Python structures and commands, such as lists and dictionaries, for the purpose of constructing neural networks because it adheres closely to the design philosophy of Python. The fact that it is both easy to use and powerful is a major contributing element to its widespread acceptance.

Tensors, which are multidimensional arrays, are at the core of PyTorch. These arrays are analogous to NumPy's ndarrays, except they have support for GPUs. Because of this GPU acceleration, efficient computation is now possible, which is very necessary when training huge neural networks, which is the foundation of deep learning.

PyTorch's built-in automatic differentiation engine, which goes by the name Autograd and is responsible for the training of neural networks, is known as the Autograd System. During the process of backpropagation, Autograd is responsible for computing the gradients or derivatives of the loss with respect to the model parameters. These values are subsequently utilized by optimization methods in order to update the weights and biases.

PyTorch's modular design promotes the explicit separation of the numerous components that make up a neural network. For example, the torch.nn module offers all of the fundamental components that are required to assemble a wide variety of neural network topologies. In a similar vein, torch.optim provides hosting for a number of different optimization techniques such as SGD and Adam.

Because PyTorch is compatible with other Python libraries, such as NumPy and SciPy, it is much simpler to deal with activities such as loading data, doing preprocessing, and visualizing the results. In addition to this, it interfaces very well with Python's multiprocessing, which makes it much simpler to employ multithreading when loading data.

PyTorch 2.0 and CUDA 11.8

With the release of PyTorch 2.0, PyTorch continues to evolve and improve. Some of the significant improvements in PyTorch 2.0 include better support for model deployment, optimizations for mobile, and tighter integration with TorchScript, allowing for more straightforward translation from research to production.

To take full advantage of the processing power of GPUs, PyTorch 2.0 leverages CUDA 11.8, a parallel computing platform and API model developed by NVIDIA. CUDA dramatically speeds up computations by allowing developers to use NVIDIA GPUs for general purpose computing, an essential requirement for handling the computational intensity of training deep neural networks. By coupling PyTorch with CUDA, developers and researchers can harness the power of the latest GPU technology to train models faster and more efficiently. This efficiency is a critical aspect of deep learning development, where model training can often be a time-consuming process.

To sum up, PyTorch is a versatile and powerful framework for deep learning. Its design philosophy - simplicity, flexibility, and efficiency, coupled with its integration with CUDA, makes it an excellent tool for developing advanced AI models. In the following chapters, we will dive into the specifics of installing PyTorch 2.0 and CUDA 11.8, and how to use these tools to build, train, and deploy neural networks.

PyTorch 2.0 Key Features

Since its inception, PyTorch has been instrumental in democratizing artificial intelligence and deep learning. With the release of PyTorch 2.0, the framework has introduced new features and improvements, reinforcing its commitment to accessibility, transparency, and performance in the field of AI.

Below are some key enhancements that PyTorch 2.0 brings to the table:

Enhanced TorchScript

TorchScript, a subset of Python used for representing PyTorch programs, has been enhanced in PyTorch 2.0. This improvement allows you to more easily transition between eager mode (PyTorch's define-by-run approach) and graph mode (define-and-run), combining the best of both worlds for increased flexibility and performance. This also allows for better optimization and serves as an important step towards improved model deployment.

Model Deployment and Serving

PyTorch 2.0 takes big strides towards facilitating better model deployment. With the introduction of TorchServe, it is now easier to take your models from the research phase to production. TorchServe provides a lightweight, robust way to serve PyTorch models, offering features like multi-model serving, model versioning, and metrics logging, among others.

Improved Mobile Support

Deep learning applications are expanding beyond servers and desktops to mobile and edge devices. Recognizing this, PyTorch 2.0 has expanded its capabilities to support the development and deployment of models on Android and iOS platforms. The PyTorch Mobile feature allows you to take your trained models and run them on mobile devices with minimal effort, enabling the development of intelligent, on-device applications.

Enhanced Quantization Support

Quantization is a technique to perform computations and storage at reduced precision. It is crucial for deploying models on devices with lower computational resources or when the network bandwidth is limited. PyTorch 2.0 introduces a native, comprehensive quantization API, providing support for both post-training and quantization-aware training. This can reduce the memory footprint of models and increase the inference speed, particularly essential for mobile or edge devices.

Named Tensors

PyTorch 2.0 introduces the concept of Named Tensors, adding naming dimensions to PyTorch's tensor representation. This can be extremely useful in complex code bases and models where it's easy to get confused with numerous dimensions and their purpose. Named tensors also improve the readability and maintainability of the code, leading to fewer bugs and errors.

Extended Ecosystem

PyTorch 2.0 benefits from an extended ecosystem of tools and libraries designed to augment and streamline various stages of model development. Libraries such as PyTorch Lightning simplify the training process, TorchText provides tools for text processing, TorchVision for image and video processing, and so forth. These libraries, compatible with PyTorch 2.0, help in creating a more cohesive and efficient development environment.

Expanded ONNX Support

Open Neural Network Exchange (ONNX) is an open standard for representing machine learning models, allowing models to be shared between different deep learning frameworks. PyTorch 2.0 improves its compatibility with ONNX, making it easier to export PyTorch models in the ONNX format, which can then be used for inference in other frameworks, or even deployed on different platforms using ONNX Runtime.

To summarize, PyTorch 2.0 carries forward the philosophy of PyTorch, offering simplicity and flexibility to its users, while introducing significant enhancements that make the transition from research to production seamless. It acknowledges the evolving needs of deep learning practitioners, paving the way for innovative, efficient, and accessible solutions in the world of AI. The subsequent chapters will delve deeper into these features, explaining how to leverage them to build and train robust deep learning models.

CUDA for Accelerated Deep Learning

In deep learning, the scale and complexity of computations involved are immense. The process of training deep neural networks involves numerous matrix multiplications and other computationally intense operations. Consequently, efficient computation becomes critical to save time and resources. This is where CUDA, or Compute Unified Device Architecture, steps in.

A Primer on CUDA

Developed by NVIDIA, CUDA is a parallel computing platform and application programming interface (API) model. It allows software developers to use NVIDIA graphics processing units (GPUs) for general-purpose computing — a practice known as GPGPU (General-Purpose computing on Graphics Processing Units). CUDA enables developers to dramatically increase the computing performance of their applications by harnessing the power of GPUs.

Why is CUDA Necessary for Deep Learning?

Because of their many-core architecture, graphics processing units (GPUs) are able to manage hundreds of threads concurrently, in contrast to central processing units (CPUs), which are only intended to handle a small number of threads at once.

The following are some of the reasons why this parallelism is especially helpful in the context of deep learning:

- Operations on Matrices: Deep learning relies heavily on linear algebra operations, many of which are extremely parallelizable, such as matrix multiplications and convolutions. GPUs are able to do these operations significantly more quickly than CPUs are because of their capacity to manage several threads at once.

- Large Datasets: When it comes to training, deep learning models typically require a significant quantity of information. GPUs are able to analyze these massive datasets more quickly, which makes the training process more effective.

- High Precision: Graphics processing units (GPUs) that have CUDA enabled may do arithmetic with a high level of precision, which is essential for preventing numerical instability during the training of deep learning models.

Blend of CUDA and PyTorch

PyTorch's integration with CUDA is one of the main reasons for its popularity in the deep learning community. The following is how this blend is beneficial:

- Seamless Integration: PyTorch offers seamless CUDA integration. Developers can leverage CUDA's parallel computing power by simply moving the computations to the GPU with minor modifications in the code.

- GPU-accelerated Tensors: PyTorch's fundamental data structure, the tensor, is compatible with GPUs. CUDA tensors, which are stored on the GPU, accelerate the operations, leading to more efficient computations.

- Multi-GPU Support: PyTorch also supports multi-GPU setups through CUDA. This allows for the parallelization of computations across multiple GPUs, further accelerating the training process.

- Autograd on GPUs: PyTorch's autograd engine, which powers its automatic differentiation and gradient computation, also works seamlessly with CUDA, ensuring that backpropagation, the backbone of neural network training, benefits from GPU acceleration.

In a nutshell, the use of CUDA in deep learning projects significantly accelerates the training process, resulting in faster model development and iteration. CUDA's blend with PyTorch provides a powerful platform for developers to build and train complex deep learning models more efficiently. As we continue our exploration of PyTorch 2.0, we'll look at how to perform these GPU-accelerated operations and build models that fully leverage the power of NVIDIA's CUDA platform.

Setting up PyTorch 2.0 and CUDA 11.8 on Linux

Before we start, it is essential that you are aware that in order to use CUDA, you will need a computer that has an NVIDIA GPU installed in it. The approach may also be slightly different for you based on the particular distribution of Linux that you are using.

We'll outline the general process as below:

Update Your System

Firstly, it's always a good idea to update your system. Open a terminal and type:

```
sudo apt-get update
sudo apt-get upgrade
```

Install Necessary Dependencies

Next, install a few necessary dependencies:

```
sudo apt-get install build-essential dkms
sudo apt-get install freeglut3 freeglut3-dev libxi-dev libxmu-dev
```

Verify CUDA-capable GPU

To verify if you have a CUDA-Capable GPU, use the following command:

```
lspci | grep -i nvidia
```

If you see output, that means you have a CUDA-capable GPU.

Download and Install CUDA 11.8

Go to the NVIDIA CUDA Downloads page. Select "Linux", then choose the appropriate options based on your Linux distribution, architecture, distribution version, and installer type (I recommend using the .run file). Then click the "Download" button to download the CUDA 11.8 toolkit.

Once downloaded, navigate to the directory containing the .run file, then run the following commands to install CUDA:

```
sudo chmod +x cuda_11.8.0_*.run
sudo ./cuda_11.8.0_*.run
```

Follow the on-screen instructions to complete the installation. Ensure to install the NVIDIA driver when prompted.

Setup Environment Variables

Next, you need to add CUDA to your path. Add these lines to your ~/.bashrc file:

```
export PATH=/usr/local/cuda-11.8/bin${PATH:+:${PATH}}
export LD_LIBRARY_PATH=/usr/local/cuda-11.8/lib64${LD_LIBRARY_PATH:+:${LD_LIBRARY_PATH}}
```

Then, source the ~/.bashrc file with the command:

```
source ~/.bashrc
```

Verify the Installation

To verify the installation, use the following command:

```
nvcc -V
```

You should see "Cuda compilation tools, release 11.8, V11.8.xxxxx" if CUDA is installed correctly.

Install PyTorch 2.0

Now, we will install PyTorch 2.0. First, we recommend creating a Python virtual environment to avoid package conflicts. Use the following commands:

```
sudo apt-get install python3-venv
python3 -m venv pytorch_env
```

```
source pytorch_env/bin/activate
```

You should see (pytorch_env) at the beginning of your command prompt, indicating you're in the virtual environment.

Now, install PyTorch using pip:

```
pip install torch==2.0.0
```

Verify PyTorch and CUDA Integration

Finally, to verify that PyTorch is properly installed and can access CUDA, run a Python interpreter and enter:

```
import torch
torch.cuda.is_available()
```

If everything is correctly installed, it should return True, indicating that PyTorch can access your GPU through CUDA. In the subsequent chapters, we'll dive into how to use this powerful setup to build and train your deep learning models.

Summary

In this opening chapter, we laid the groundwork for understanding deep learning, neural networks, PyTorch 2.0, and CUDA 11.8. We started with a comprehensive overview of neural networks, highlighting their core structure composed of neurons and layers. We delved into their vital role in deep learning, facilitating the learning from vast volumes of data and the complex computations involved. Neural networks' power comes from their ability to learn representations and make predictions from data, a cornerstone of deep learning.

We then moved on to introducing PyTorch 2.0, a widely used deep learning framework known for its flexibility, user-friendly interface, and efficient computation capabilities. PyTorch 2.0 carries forward its legacy, while introducing numerous enhancements. Its key features include enhanced TorchScript for a more flexible programming model, improved model deployment with TorchServe, better mobile support, comprehensive quantization support, named tensors for better code readability, and an extended ecosystem of tools and libraries.

Finally, we discussed the significance of CUDA for deep learning, which allows for significant acceleration of training processes by harnessing the parallel computing capabilities of NVIDIA GPUs. We also highlighted the seamless blend of CUDA with PyTorch that enables efficient computations and speedy model training. Concluding the chapter, we walked through the step-by-step setup of a PyTorch 2.0 and CUDA 11.8 environment on a Linux platform. This setup allows developers to fully leverage the power of GPU-accelerated operations in their deep learning projects, setting the stage for subsequent chapters where we will delve deeper into practical applications.

CHAPTER 2: GETTING STARTED WITH TENSORS

Diving into Tensors

A tensor, in the context of deep learning, is a generalization of vectors and matrices to potentially higher dimensions, and is a fundamental data structure in PyTorch. Tensors are a type of data structure used in linear algebra, and like vectors and matrices, you can calculate arithmetic operations with tensors.

Understanding Tensors

Tensors are a core unit of data in PyTorch and are represented as multi-dimensional arrays. The dimensionality of a tensor can be described with rank, shape, and size.

- Rank: This simply tells us the number of dimensions in a tensor. A scalar has rank 0, a vector has rank 1, a matrix has rank 2, and a tensor has rank 3 or more.

- Shape: The shape of a tensor is the number of elements in each dimension.

- Size: The total number of items in the tensor, which can be computed as a product of the elements of the shape.

In PyTorch, tensors allow for operations to be performed on GPUs, which can significantly accelerate the computations. They are similar to NumPy's ndarrays, with the addition being that Tensors can also be used on a GPU to accelerate computing.

Different Tensors

PyTorch provides various functions to create different types of tensors. Below are a few examples:

- Empty Tensor: torch.empty(size): Returns a tensor of given size filled with uninitialized data. Here, size is a tuple defining the dimension of the tensor.

- Zero Tensor: torch.zeros(size): Returns a tensor filled with zeroes.

- Ones Tensor: torch.ones(size): Returns a tensor filled with ones.

- Random Tensor: torch.rand(size): Returns a tensor filled with random numbers from a uniform distribution in the range [0, 1).

Tensor Terminologies and Concepts

Tensors, the multi-dimensional generalization of scalars, vectors, and matrices, are key to the functionality of PyTorch, a popular deep learning framework. Mastering the concepts associated with tensors is a vital step in harnessing the full power of PyTorch, as these data structures are pivotal for efficiently carrying out computations in deep learning.

Scalar

A scalar is the simplest type of tensor, containing only a single element with no dimensions. When translated into the PyTorch framework, a scalar can be represented as torch.tensor(5). This is a tensor with zero dimensions, a concept that's akin to a point in the realm of geometry – having a position, but lacking extent.

Vector

A vector, on the other hand, is a one-dimensional tensor, similar to a line in geometry. An example of a vector in PyTorch would be torch.tensor([1, 2, 3, 4]). This tensor has a single axis and therefore has an extent or length, with each element corresponding to a point along that axis.

Matrix

Advancing in complexity, a matrix is a two-dimensional tensor, possessing both rows and columns. In PyTorch, it could be represented as torch.tensor([[1, 2], [3, 4]]). Matrices can be thought of as a table of numbers or a grid that spans two directions or axes.

Tensor Operations

An essential aspect of tensor manipulation is the numerous tensor operations supported by PyTorch. These operations cover a broad spectrum, ranging from basic arithmetic operations like addition, subtraction, multiplication, and division to more complex linear algebra functions. Element-wise operations, reduction operations, and comparison operations form a rich palette of tools that make PyTorch an effective and versatile platform for deep learning tasks.

Broadcasting

An especially powerful mechanism of PyTorch is broadcasting, a functionality that allows the framework to deal with arrays of different shapes during arithmetic operations. It extends smaller arrays to match larger ones, allowing element-wise operations to be conducted smoothly, a feature that significantly enhances the flexibility and convenience of array manipulations.

Device

Finally, the 'Device' aspect of PyTorch ensures that tensors can be seamlessly moved to any device memory using the .to method. For example, tensor.to("cuda") facilitates the transfer of the tensor to the GPU, thus enabling hardware-accelerated computations, which are crucial in handling the massive computational demands of deep learning.

Tensors are the backbone of PyTorch and thus, understanding them is pivotal to effectively leverage the PyTorch framework. They provide the computational efficiency that deep learning algorithms need to process vast amounts of data and perform complex computations. This fundamental understanding sets the stage for more advanced concepts and techniques in deep learning that we will explore in subsequent chapters.

Sample Program to Create Tensors

We will dive into creating tensors using PyTorch. We'll see how to create an empty tensor, tensors filled with ones, zeros, and random values. Please be informed, you must have PyTorch installed to run these codes.

Firstly, we will import the PyTorch library:

```
import torch
```

Creating an Empty Tensor:

```
empty_tensor = torch.empty(3, 2)
print(empty_tensor)
```

This will create a tensor of shape 3x2 filled with uninitialized data. The output will be something like:

```
tensor([[2.1019e-44, 0.0000e+00],
        [      nan, 0.0000e+00],
        [1.3733e-14, 6.4069e+02]])
```

Creating a Tensor Filled with Zeros:

```python
zero_tensor = torch.zeros(3, 2)
print(zero_tensor)
```

This will create a tensor of shape 3x2 filled with zeros. The output will be:

```
tensor([[0., 0.],
        [0., 0.],
        [0., 0.]])
```

Creating a Tensor Filled with Ones:

```python
ones_tensor = torch.ones(3, 2)
print(ones_tensor)
```

This will create a tensor of shape 3x2 filled with ones. The output will be:

```
tensor([[1., 1.],
        [1., 1.],
        [1., 1.]])
```

Creating a Random Tensor:

```python
random_tensor = torch.rand(3, 2)
print(random_tensor)
```

This will create a tensor of shape 3x2 filled with random numbers from a uniform distribution on the interval [0, 1). The output will be something like:

```
tensor([[0.6022, 0.9622],
        [0.7817, 0.5994],
        [0.6712, 0.4674]])
```

These basic tensor operations form the building blocks for creating more complex data structures in PyTorch, which is instrumental when modeling neural networks and developing deep learning applications.

Tensor Data Types

In PyTorch, tensors have associated data types similar to data types in Python. This data type defines the kind of elements that are contained within the tensor and the possible range of their values.

Below are some of the most commonly used data types:
- torch.float32 or torch.float: 32-bit floating point
- torch.float64 or torch.double: 64-bit, double-precision floating-point
- torch.float16 or torch.half: 16-bit, half-precision floating-point
- torch.int32 or torch.int: 32-bit integer (signed)
- torch.int64 or torch.long: 64-bit integer (signed)
- torch.bool: Boolean type

The default data type for tensors is 32-bit floating point. You can change the data type of a tensor using the .to() method.

We will see this in action:

```python
# Import PyTorch
import torch

# Create tensor with default data type (float32)
tensor = torch.ones(3, 2)
print(tensor)
print("Data Type: ", tensor.dtype)

# Changing tensor data type to float64
tensor = tensor.to(torch.float64)
print("\nAfter Changing Data Type to float64:")
print(tensor)
print("Data Type: ", tensor.dtype)

# Changing tensor data type to int32
```

```python
tensor = tensor.to(torch.int32)
print("\nAfter Changing Data Type to int32:")
print(tensor)
print("Data Type: ", tensor.dtype)

# Changing tensor data type to boolean
tensor = tensor.to(torch.bool)
print("\nAfter Changing Data Type to boolean:")
print(tensor)
print("Data Type: ", tensor.dtype)
```

The output will be:

```
tensor([[1., 1.],
        [1., 1.],
        [1., 1.]])
Data Type:  torch.float32

After Changing Data Type to float64:

tensor([[1., 1.],
        [1., 1.],
        [1., 1.]], dtype=torch.float64)
Data Type:  torch.float64

After Changing Data Type to int32:

tensor([[1, 1],
        [1, 1],
        [1, 1]], dtype=torch.int32)
Data Type:  torch.int32

After Changing Data Type to boolean:
```

tensor([[True, True],
    [True, True],
    [True, True]])
Data Type: torch.bool

It's also worth mentioning that PyTorch provides a function to create a tensor of a specific type, for example: torch.zeros(3,2,dtype=torch.int32). It's also crucial to ensure tensors used in calculations are of the same type, as PyTorch does not perform implicit type conversion.

Understanding and properly managing tensor data types is an essential aspect of developing robust and efficient deep learning models in PyTorch.

Standard Arithmetic Operations

We will see how to perform basic arithmetic operations on tensors. We will cover addition, subtraction, multiplication, and division operations.

Firstly, we will create two tensors of the same shape:

```python
# Import PyTorch
import torch

# Create two tensors
tensor1 = torch.tensor([1, 2, 3, 4], dtype=torch.float32)
tensor2 = torch.tensor([5, 6, 7, 8], dtype=torch.float32)

print("Tensor 1:", tensor1)
print("Tensor 2:", tensor2)
```

Output:

```
Tensor 1: tensor([1., 2., 3., 4.])
Tensor 2: tensor([5., 6., 7., 8.])
```

Addition

```
# Addition
result = tensor1 + tensor2
print("Addition Result: ", result)
```

Output:

```
Addition Result:  tensor([ 6.,  8., 10., 12.])
```

Subtraction

```
# Subtraction
result = tensor1 - tensor2
print("Subtraction Result: ", result)
```

Output:

```
Subtraction Result:  tensor([-4., -4., -4., -4.])
```

Multiplication

```
# Multiplication (Element-wise)
result = tensor1 * tensor2
print("Multiplication Result: ", result)
```

Output:

```
Multiplication Result:  tensor([ 5., 12., 21., 32.])
```

Division

```python
# Division
result = tensor1 / tensor2
print("Division Result: ", result)
```

Output:

```
Division Result:  tensor([0.2000, 0.3333, 0.4286, 0.5000])
```

Please be informed that the operations are element-wise, meaning they are applied on corresponding elements of the two tensors.

These standard operations are fundamental for manipulating tensors and implementing various mathematical models, especially in the fields of machine learning and deep learning. Next, we'll get into more complex operations and explore how these basic operations can be combined to implement more complex computations.

Tensor Manipulation

Tensor manipulation in PyTorch typically involves operations like reshaping, slicing, and joining tensors. We will delve into each of these topics.

Reshaping Tensors

Reshaping tensors is a common operation, which allows us to restructure our data to have different numbers of dimensions or different sizes for each dimension.

We will create a tensor and then reshape it:

```python
# Import PyTorch
import torch

# Create a tensor
tensor = torch.arange(9)
print("Original Tensor:")
print(tensor)
```

```python
# Reshape the tensor
reshaped_tensor = tensor.view(3, 3)
print("\nReshaped Tensor:")
print(reshaped_tensor)
```

Output:

```
Original Tensor:
tensor([0, 1, 2, 3, 4, 5, 6, 7, 8])

Reshaped Tensor:
tensor([[0, 1, 2],
        [3, 4, 5],
        [6, 7, 8]])
```

Slicing Tensors

Slicing allows us to extract a portion of the tensor. The slicing syntax in PyTorch is quite similar to that in Python and NumPy.

```python
# Slicing the tensor
sliced_tensor = reshaped_tensor[0:2, 0:2]
print("\nSliced Tensor:")
print(sliced_tensor)
```

Output:

```
Sliced Tensor:
tensor([[0, 1],
        [3, 4]])
```

Joining Tensors

PyTorch provides several methods to combine tensors, such as torch.cat() and torch.stack(). We will use torch.cat() to concatenate two tensors along a given dimension:

```python
# Create two tensors
tensor1 = torch.tensor([1, 2, 3])
tensor2 = torch.tensor([4, 5, 6])

# Concatenate the tensors along dimension 0
concatenated_tensor = torch.cat((tensor1, tensor2))
print("\nConcatenated Tensor:")
print(concatenated_tensor)
```

Output:

```
Concatenated Tensor:
tensor([1, 2, 3, 4, 5, 6])
```

These operations are foundational for tensor manipulation. Mastery of these concepts will enable you to effectively work with tensors and prepare your data for deep learning models.

Matrix Multiplication

In PyTorch, you can perform matrix multiplication using the torch.matmul() function or the @ operator. Both of these methods check the dimensionality of the tensors and apply the appropriate multiplication operation (element-wise multiplication for 1D tensors, matrix multiplication for 2D tensors, batched matrix multiplication for 3D tensors).

We will create two matrices and perform a matrix multiplication operation.

```python
# Import PyTorch
import torch

# Create two 2D tensors (matrices)
matrix1 = torch.tensor([[1, 2], [3, 4]])
matrix2 = torch.tensor([[5, 6], [7, 8]])

print("Matrix 1:")
print(matrix1)
```

```python
print("\nMatrix 2:")
print(matrix2)

# Matrix multiplication using torch.matmul()
result = torch.matmul(matrix1, matrix2)
print("\nMatrix Multiplication Result using torch.matmul():")
print(result)

# Matrix multiplication using @ operator
result = matrix1 @ matrix2
print("\nMatrix Multiplication Result using @ operator:")
print(result)
```

Output:

```
Matrix 1:
tensor([[1, 2],
        [3, 4]])

Matrix 2:
tensor([[5, 6],
        [7, 8]])

Matrix Multiplication Result using torch.matmul():
tensor([[19, 22],
        [43, 50]])

Matrix Multiplication Result using @ operator:
tensor([[19, 22],
        [43, 50]])
```

The result of the multiplication operation is calculated by the dot product of rows from the first matrix and columns from the second matrix. This operation is fundamental in linear algebra and is frequently used in deep learning, for instance, when propagating inputs through the layers of a neural network.

When multiplying matrices, it is important to keep in mind that the number of rows in the second matrix must be equal to the number of columns in the first matrix.

Manage Tensor Shape Errors

In PyTorch, dealing with tensor shape errors often requires understanding the nature of the operation you're performing and the dimensionality of your tensors. Below are a few common cases where you might encounter shape errors:

Matrix Multiplication

If you're doing matrix multiplication, the number of columns in the first matrix must equal the number of rows in the second matrix. If this condition is not satisfied, you'll encounter a size mismatch error.

For example:

```
matrix1 = torch.rand(2, 3)
matrix2 = torch.rand(2, 3)
result = torch.matmul(matrix1, matrix2)  # This will raise a size mismatch error
```

In the above example, reshaping or transposing matrix2 will resolve the issue:

```
matrix2 = matrix2.t()  # Transpose the matrix
result = torch.matmul(matrix1, matrix2)  # This will not raise an error
```

Element-wise Operations

If you're doing element-wise operations (like addition, subtraction, etc.), the tensors involved should have the same shape. PyTorch does support broadcasting (a concept borrowed from NumPy), which allows for binary operations on tensors of different sizes, but there are rules to this as well.

For example:

```python
tensor1 = torch.rand(2, 3)
tensor2 = torch.rand(2, 2)
result = tensor1 + tensor2  # This will raise a size mismatch error
```

In the above case, ensuring both tensors have the same shape will fix the error.

Reshaping Tensors

If you're reshaping a tensor, the total number of elements before and after the reshape operation should remain the same. If this isn't the case, you'll encounter an error.

For example:

```python
tensor = torch.rand(2, 3)
reshaped_tensor = tensor.view(2, 4)  # This will raise an error
```

In the above case, ensuring the new shape is compatible with the number of elements in the tensor will solve the problem.

Whenever you encounter a shape error, carefully examine the dimensions of the tensors you're working with and the requirements of the operations you're performing. Use methods like .size() or .shape to inspect the size of your tensors and view(), reshape(), or transpose() to manipulate the shape of your tensors when needed.

Aggregation Operations

Aggregation operations in PyTorch are those that reduce the number of elements contained within a tensor. These include operations like finding the sum, mean, maximum, or minimum of the elements.

We will create a tensor and perform various aggregation operations:

```python
# Import PyTorch
import torch


# Create a tensor
tensor = torch.tensor([[1, 2, 3], [4, 5, 6]], dtype=torch.float32)
```

```python
print("Tensor:")
print(tensor)
```

Output:

```
Tensor:
tensor([[1., 2., 3.],
        [4., 5., 6.]])
```

Sum

Find the sum of all elements in the tensor:

```python
# Sum of tensor
sum_val = torch.sum(tensor)
print("\nSum of Tensor Elements: ", sum_val)
```

Output:

```
Sum of Tensor Elements:  tensor(21.)
```

Mean

Compute the mean of the tensor elements:

```python
# Mean of tensor
mean_val = torch.mean(tensor)
print("\nMean of Tensor Elements: ", mean_val)
```

Output:

```
Mean of Tensor Elements:  tensor(3.5)
```

Max

Find the maximum value in the tensor:

```python
# Max of tensor
max_val = torch.max(tensor)
print("\nMax of Tensor Elements: ", max_val)
```

Output:

```
Max of Tensor Elements:  tensor(6.)
```

Min

Find the minimum value in the tensor:

```python
# Min of tensor
min_val = torch.min(tensor)
print("\nMin of Tensor Elements: ", min_val)
```

Output:

```
Min of Tensor Elements:  tensor(1.)
```

These operations are often used in machine learning for tasks like normalization, finding the maximum prediction value, and more. Being able to perform aggregations on tensors is a critical skill when working with PyTorch.

Keep thinking about that the torch.mean() function can only be executed on tensors that use floating point values. If the data in your tensor is of the integer type, the first thing you'll need to do is convert it to the float type.

Summary

In this chapter, we delved deeper into the essential building block of PyTorch: the tensor. We started by understanding what tensors are, their significance, and how they are fundamental to the operations in PyTorch and deep learning in general. Tensors, in essence, are a generalization of matrices to multiple dimensions, and they are the primary data structure used in PyTorch. They are similar to NumPy's ndarrays but with added GPU support.

We then explored creating and manipulating tensors. We saw how to instantiate tensors of various types, like zeroes, ones, or random tensors, and how to specify their data types. We learned about operations on tensors, which included reshaping, slicing, and joining tensors, all of which are essential for data preprocessing and transformation in machine learning workflows. We then learned about performing basic arithmetic operations on tensors, matrix multiplication, and the concept of broadcasting, which allows us to perform operations between tensors of different shapes.

Lastly, we delved into handling tensor shape errors, which is a common challenge when working with tensor-based computations. We learned that understanding the dimensionality of our tensors and the requirements of the operations we're performing is crucial to preventing and resolving such errors. We also covered aggregation operations on tensors, such as finding the sum, mean, maximum, or minimum of tensor elements. These operations are fundamental in various machine learning tasks.

Chapter 3: Advanced Tensor Operations

Advanced Tensor Operations Overview

The ability to manipulate and manage tensors is fundamental to the use of PyTorch and other similar deep learning frameworks. Tensors are at the core of everything we do in PyTorch, and they're used to encode the inputs and outputs of models, as well as the model's parameters.

Reshaping

Reshaping a tensor refers to the process of changing its dimensions while keeping the underlying data intact. It's akin to rearranging the layout of data without altering the data points themselves. This technique becomes extremely useful while preparing data for certain types of models, as different models require inputs in different dimensions. For instance, convolutional neural networks typically expect a 4D tensor as input - represented as (Batch Size x Channels x Height x Width). In such cases, if the original data is in a 2D format (Height x Width), reshaping can convert it to the required 4D format without any data loss or alteration.

Viewing

Viewing is another key aspect of tensor management in PyTorch. The view() function is primarily used to reshape tensors, similar to the way the reshape() function operates. However, view() has a unique feature where it can automatically infer the correct size for one dimension based on the sizes of the other dimensions. This capability is particularly beneficial when the size of one dimension is known, but PyTorch is required to calculate the size of the other dimensions. This inferencing feature simplifies the reshaping process, making it more efficient and less error-prone.

Stacking

Stacking is yet another technique used for managing tensors. Stacking allows us to combine several tensors along a new dimension, creating a higher-dimensional tensor. It is frequently used to create batches of inputs or targets, but it also serves as a general-purpose tool for concatenating results. For instance, suppose there's a need to amalgamate a list of tensors into a single tensor. In that case, the stack() function can be employed. This operation effectively stacks the input tensors like pancakes, creating a new dimension in the process. For example, stacking three 2D tensors would result in a 3D tensor.

Understanding each of these operations and knowing when to use each one is essential for developing deep learning models. It can greatly speed up the data preparation process, make your code more readable, and can also help avoid bugs or issues down the line. These operations give us the flexibility we need to handle a wide range of different tasks, and as such, they are a vital part of any PyTorch developer's toolkit.

Changing Shape of Tensor

In PyTorch, reshape() is used to change the shape of a tensor without changing its data. This operation is commonly used when you want to rearrange the dimensions of your data to match the input expectations of a model.

```python
# Import PyTorch
import torch

# Create a tensor
tensor = torch.arange(1, 9)
print("Original Tensor:")
print(tensor)

# Reshape the tensor
reshaped_tensor = tensor.reshape(2, 4)
print("\nReshaped Tensor:")
print(reshaped_tensor)
```

Output:

```
Original Tensor:
tensor([1, 2, 3, 4, 5, 6, 7, 8])

Reshaped Tensor:
tensor([[1, 2, 3, 4],
        [5, 6, 7, 8]])
```

Viewing Tensor Dimensions

The view() function is similar to reshape(), but it operates as an in-place operation, and it can infer the size of a dimension by using -1. If the tensor is not contiguous, you may have to use reshape() or call contiguous() before using view().

```
# View the tensor
viewed_tensor = tensor.view(2, 4)
print("\nViewed Tensor:")
print(viewed_tensor)
```

Output:

```
Viewed Tensor:
tensor([[1, 2, 3, 4],
        [5, 6, 7, 8]])
```

Stacking Sequence of Tensors

The stack() function is used to concatenate a sequence of tensors along a new dimension. All tensors need to be of the same size.

```
# Create two tensors
tensor1 = torch.tensor([1, 2, 3])
tensor2 = torch.tensor([4, 5, 6])

# Stack the tensors
stacked_tensor = torch.stack((tensor1, tensor2))
print("\nStacked Tensor:")
print(stacked_tensor)
```

Output:

```
Stacked Tensor:
tensor([[1, 2, 3],
        [4, 5, 6]])
```

These advanced tensor operations are fundamental for managing and manipulating your data effectively in PyTorch. Understanding these operations will allow you to structure your data in a way that's compatible with your models.

Squeezing a Tensor

The squeeze() function removes the dimensions or axes that have a length of one from the tensor. This operation is useful to transform a 2D tensor with one dimension of length 1 into a 1D tensor, or to remove unnecessary dimensions when you have a batch size of 1.

```python
# Create a tensor of size (1,3)
tensor = torch.zeros((1, 3))
print("Original Tensor:")
print(tensor)
print("Shape:", tensor.shape)

# Squeeze the tensor
squeezed_tensor = tensor.squeeze()
print("\nSqueezed Tensor:")
print(squeezed_tensor)
print("Shape:", squeezed_tensor.shape)
```

Output:

```
Original Tensor:
tensor([[0., 0., 0.]])
Shape: torch.Size([1, 3])

Squeezed Tensor:
tensor([0., 0., 0.])
Shape: torch.Size([3])
```

Un-squeezing a Tensor

unsqueeze() is the inverse operation to squeeze(). It adds a dimension with a length of one at the specified position in the tensor. This is commonly used to increase the dimensionality of your data to match the input requirements of a model.

```
# Unsqueeze the tensor
unsqueezed_tensor = squeezed_tensor.unsqueeze(dim=0)
print("\nUnsqueezed Tensor:")
print(unsqueezed_tensor)
print("Shape:", unsqueezed_tensor.shape)
```

Output:

```
Unsqueezed Tensor:
tensor([[0., 0., 0.]])
Shape: torch.Size([1, 3])
```

Permuting a Tensor

The permute() function rearranges the original dimensions of the tensor according to the input specified. It's often used to change the order of the dimensions or axes.

```
# Create a tensor of size (2, 3, 4)
tensor = torch.zeros((2, 3, 4))
print("\nOriginal Tensor Shape:", tensor.shape)

# Permute the dimensions of the tensor
permuted_tensor = tensor.permute(2, 0, 1)
print("Permuted Tensor Shape:", permuted_tensor.shape)
```

Output:

```
Original Tensor Shape: torch.Size([2, 3, 4])
Permuted Tensor Shape: torch.Size([4, 2, 3])
```

In the permute example above, the original tensor's dimensions were (2, 3, 4), corresponding to indices (0, 1, 2). We permuted the tensor to the new dimensions (4, 2, 3), so the original third dimension (of size 4) is now the first, the first is now the second, and the second is now the third.

Understanding these tensor operations is fundamental when handling multi-dimensional data and ensuring it fits the specific input requirements of your models.

Indexing and Selecting Data from Tensors

Indexing and selecting data from tensors is an essential operation when working with PyTorch and the process closely resembles how indexing works with standard Python lists or NumPy arrays. This operation uses square brackets [] to access specific elements or subsets of data within the tensor.

To select a specific element in a tensor, you can use an integer index. For instance, if 'x' is a one-dimensional tensor, you could use x[0] to select the first element. Similarly, x[-1] would select the last element. For multi-dimensional tensors, you can use a comma-separated tuple of indices. If 'y' is a two-dimensional tensor, y[1,2] would give the element at the second row and third column.

We will continue with some examples:

```
# Import PyTorch
import torch


# Create a tensor
tensor = torch.tensor([[1, 2, 3], [4, 5, 6], [7, 8, 9]])
print("Original Tensor:")
print(tensor)
```

Output:

```
Original Tensor:
tensor([[1, 2, 3],
        [4, 5, 6],
        [7, 8, 9]])
```

Indexing a Tensor

You can access a specific element in the tensor by its index. Remember, indexing starts at 0 in Python:

```python
# Get the element at row 1, column 2
element = tensor[1, 2]
print("\nElement at Row 1, Column 2: ", element)
```

Output:

```
Element at Row 1, Column 2:  tensor(6)
```

Slicing a Tensor

You can also select a range of elements using slicing:

```python
# Get the elements in row 0 and 1
rows = tensor[0:2]
print("\nElements in Row 0 and 1:")
print(rows)
```

Output:

```
Elements in Row 0 and 1:
tensor([[1, 2, 3],
        [4, 5, 6]])
```

Selecting Specific Indices

For more complex selection, you can use the index_select() method to select data by specific indices:

```python
# Create an index tensor
indices = torch.tensor([0, 2])
```

```python
# Select rows at indices 0 and 2
selected_rows = tensor.index_select(0, indices)
print("\nSelected Rows at Indices 0 and 2:")
print(selected_rows)
```

Output:

```
Selected Rows at Indices 0 and 2:
tensor([[1, 2, 3],
        [7, 8, 9]])
```

In the index_select() function, the first argument is the dimension along which to index (0 for rows, 1 for columns in a 2D tensor), and the second argument is the tensor containing the indices.

These tensor indexing operations are crucial when working with data in machine learning, allowing you to select and manipulate specific portions of your datasets.

Switching Access Between GPU and CPU

In PyTorch, tensors can live either on the CPU or on the GPU, and switching between the two is done with the .to() method. Before diving into the details, we will discuss why this is necessary.

Necessity of Access of Choice

The primary reason to switch between CPU and GPU lies in the type of computations you're performing. The GPU is well-suited for computations involving large amounts of data (like those in deep learning), as it can perform many computations simultaneously. On the other hand, the CPU is better suited for tasks requiring less data but more complex or conditional operations. By enabling you to switch between CPU and GPU, PyTorch lets you write code that can run on different hardware and that optimizes for their specific advantages.

The following is an example of how you can use the .to() method:

```python
# Import PyTorch
```

```python
import torch

# Create a tensor
tensor = torch.tensor([1, 2, 3])
print("Original tensor:")
print(tensor)

# Check the current device of the tensor
print("\nTensor is on: ", tensor.device)

# Move the tensor to GPU if available
if torch.cuda.is_available():
    tensor = tensor.to('cuda')

print("\nMoved tensor:")
print(tensor)
print("Tensor is on: ", tensor.device)
```

In the above sample program, we start by creating a tensor on the CPU (which is the default device). We then check whether a GPU is available using torch.cuda.is_available(). If a GPU is available, we move our tensor to the GPU using .to('cuda').

Device-agnostic code means that the code can run on any device without modification. The following is an example of how you can achieve this in PyTorch:

```python
# Define the device
device = torch.device("cuda" if torch.cuda.is_available() else "cpu")

# Create a tensor directly on the target device
tensor = torch.tensor([1, 2, 3], device=device)
print("Tensor is on: ", tensor.device)
```

By defining the device at the beginning of the script and using it whenever you create a tensor, you can ensure your code runs on the GPU if available, and falls back to the CPU if not. This makes your code device-agnostic, as it can utilize any available hardware without requiring modification.

Summary

In this chapter, we delved into advanced operations for manipulating and managing tensors in PyTorch. The first section introduced reshaping, viewing, and stacking of tensors. Reshaping allows us to change the shape of the tensor without modifying the underlying data, while viewing offers a similar function with the ability to infer a dimension size using -1. Stacking concatenates a sequence of tensors along a new dimension, provided all tensors are of the same size. These operations are fundamental for effectively managing our data in PyTorch, helping us structure our data to be compatible with our models.

Next, we discussed squeezing, unsqueezing, and permuting tensors. Squeezing removes dimensions with a length of one, which often proves useful in shedding unneeded dimensions when the batch size is one. Conversely, unsqueezing adds a dimension with a length of one at the specified position, frequently used to match the model's input requirements. Permutation is used to rearrange the original tensor's dimensions according to the input specified, commonly used to change the order of dimensions or axes. Understanding these operations is crucial when working with multi-dimensional data, ensuring it fits our models' specific input requirements.

The final sections introduced us to tensor indexing, selection, and device-agnostic coding. Tensor indexing and selection in PyTorch follow similar principles as with Python lists and NumPy arrays, allowing us to manipulate and select specific portions of our datasets. We learned to use square brackets for indexing and slicing, and the index_select() method for more complex selection. The necessity of switching between CPU and GPU was discussed, with an introduction to the .to() method. Device-agnostic code can run on different hardware, optimizing for their specific advantages. By defining the device at the beginning of the script, our code can utilize any available hardware without modification. This flexibility is crucial for machine learning, where the computational resources may vary greatly across different environments.

Chapter 4: Building Neural Networks with PyTorch 2.0

PyTorch NN Module Overview

This chapter dives deep into the realm of PyTorch's nn module - a module crucial for building neural networks. As PyTorch's core package for neural networks, nn depends on autograd to define and compute gradients, making it greatly flexible and intuitive.

At the heart of nn are layers, which are nothing more than simple mathematical functions structured in a way to learn from the data. A typical neural network consists of a sequence of layers, where each layer takes the output from the previous layer as its input. For example, a simple fully connected (or dense) layer, also known as a linear layer, applies a linear transformation to its input, while a convolutional layer applies a convolution operation. The nn module includes a variety of layers such as nn.Linear, nn.Conv2d, and nn.MaxPool2d to name a few.

Activation functions are another essential component of neural networks. They introduce non-linear properties to the network, enabling it to learn from complex data. Without activation functions, a neural network would simply be a linear regression model, unable to learn from intricate patterns. Common activation functions include the ReLU (Rectified Linear Unit), Sigmoid, and Tanh. In PyTorch, these are readily available as nn.ReLU, nn.Sigmoid, and nn.Tanh.

Loss functions, also known as cost functions, measure how far the network's predictions are from the actual values. During training, the aim is to minimize this loss. Different types of loss functions are suitable for different types of tasks. For instance, Mean Squared Error (nn.MSELoss) is commonly used for regression problems, while Cross Entropy Loss (nn.CrossEntropyLoss) is used for multi-class classification problems.

Choosing the right combination of layers, activation functions, and loss functions for your network architecture is essential to a successful deep learning project. Making these choices typically requires a mixture of domain knowledge, intuition, and empirical testing. PyTorch's nn module, with its rich assortment of layers and utilities, provides the tools needed to construct virtually any neural network architecture, from a simple linear model to complex structures like transformers or recurrent networks. By fully understanding and leveraging the capabilities of the nn module, you can effectively harness the power of deep learning.

Understanding Feedforward Networks

Overview

Feedforward networks, often simply referred to as neural networks, form the backbone of many modern machine learning models. They are called "feedforward" because information travels through them in one direction: from the input layer, through any number of hidden layers, to the output layer. No information loops back within the network, which differentiates them from recurrent neural networks where such loops are allowed.

A basic feedforward network consists of at least three types of layers: an input layer, which receives the initial data; one or more hidden layers, where the actual processing is done via a system of weighted connections; and an output layer, which produces the final result. Each layer consists of multiple neurons (also called nodes), and each neuron in a layer is connected to all neurons in the previous and next layers. The "depth" of a neural network refers to the number of hidden layers it has.

Advantages of Feedforward Networks

One of the primary advantages of feedforward networks is their ability to model complex non-linear relationships. By adjusting the weights and biases of the connections through a process called "backpropagation" and the optimization of a loss function, a feedforward network can learn non-linear relationships between its inputs and outputs. This is the primary feature that distinguishes neural networks from simpler linear models.

Feedforward networks are also highly flexible and can be adapted to many types of predictive modeling problems. They can be used for tasks as diverse as image classification, speech recognition, natural language processing, and even game playing. The flexibility extends to handling different types of data, including text, images, sound, and numerical data.

Additionally, feedforward networks can be used to learn representations of data in the hidden layers, which can then be used for dimensionality reduction or exploratory data analysis. This feature is useful in unsupervised learning, where the goal is to discover inherent structures within the data.

Feedforward networks also benefit from the continual advancements in computational resources and techniques. The development of hardware accelerators like GPUs and TPUs has vastly increased the speed and efficiency of training large and deep neural networks. Additionally, optimization techniques like stochastic gradient descent (SGD), RMSProp, and Adam have made the training process more efficient.

However, despite these benefits, feedforward networks do have some limitations. They require substantial amounts of data and computational resources to train effectively, particularly as the size and complexity of the network increases. Also, the model's "black box" nature makes it difficult to interpret how it arrived at a particular output, which can be problematic in contexts where interpretability is important.

To sum up, feedforward networks are a powerful tool in the machine learning toolbox. They offer the ability to model complex non-linear relationships and the flexibility to adapt to a wide range of tasks and data types. Despite their limitations, they have proven their worth in countless practical applications, making them an indispensable asset in modern machine learning.

Build Multi-layer Perceptron using PyTorch

The process of creating a feedforward network (also known as a multi-layer perceptron or MLP) in PyTorch involves several steps. Below, we walk through these steps, detailing how each part of the network is constructed and fits together:

Import the necessary libraries: First, you'll need to import PyTorch and the torch.nn module, which contains the necessary building blocks for neural networks.

```
import torch
from torch import nn
```

Define the network architecture: To define a feedforward network, we subclass nn.Module, PyTorch's base class for all neural network modules. Within our new class, we define the layers of our network in the constructor and specify how data should be passed through the network in the forward method.

The following is an example of a simple feedforward network with one hidden layer:

```
class FeedforwardNetwork(nn.Module):
    def __init__(self, input_size, hidden_size, output_size):
        super(FeedforwardNetwork, self).__init__()
        self.hidden = nn.Linear(input_size, hidden_size)  # Hidden layer
        self.relu = nn.ReLU()  # Non-linear activation function
```

```python
        self.output = nn.Linear(hidden_size, output_size)  # Output layer

    def forward(self, x):
        out = self.hidden(x)
        out = self.relu(out)
        out = self.output(out)
        return out
```

In this network, input_size is the number of features in the input data, hidden_size is the number of neurons in the hidden layer, and output_size is the number of neurons in the output layer (which should match the number of classes for a classification task, or be 1 for a regression task).

Instantiate the network: Once the architecture is defined, you can create an instance of your network by providing the required dimensions.

```python
input_size = 10  # for example
hidden_size = 50  # for example
output_size = 1  # for example
model = FeedforwardNetwork(input_size, hidden_size, output_size)
```

Define the loss function and the optimizer: The next step is to define the loss function and the optimizer. The loss function measures how far the network's predictions are from the actual values. The optimizer is used to adjust the weights of the network to minimize the loss.

```python
criterion = nn.MSELoss()  # for example
optimizer = torch.optim.Adam(model.parameters())
```

Train the network: Finally, you can train the network using your training data. In each epoch (full pass through the training data), the model makes a prediction, calculates the loss, and updates the weights.

```python
for epoch in range(num_epochs):
    # Forward pass
```

```
outputs = model(inputs)
loss = criterion(outputs, labels)

# Backward and optimize
optimizer.zero_grad()
loss.backward()
optimizer.step()
```

This is a simple demonstration of a feedforward network in PyTorch. The actual network might have multiple hidden layers, different activation functions, different types of layers (e.g., convolutional, recurrent), and other complexities depending on the specific task.

Understanding Recurrent Neural Networks

Overview

Recurrent Neural Networks (RNNs) are a class of neural networks that are specially designed to handle sequential data. Unlike feedforward networks, which process inputs independently, RNNs have internal loops that allow information to be passed from one step in the sequence to the next. This ability to persist information makes them ideal for tasks involving time series data, natural language processing, speech recognition, and more.

To delve a bit deeper, RNNs introduce the concept of a hidden state that holds information about past inputs in the sequence. During each step in the sequence, the hidden state is updated based on the current input and the previous hidden state. This allows the network to retain information from earlier in the sequence and use it to influence later outputs. Theoretically, RNNs can remember information from any point in the past. However, in practice, RNNs have difficulty maintaining long-term dependencies due to the vanishing gradient problem, wherein the gradients of the loss function become increasingly small as they are propagated back through time. This can make it hard for the network to learn from experiences that occurred many time steps in the past.

There are specialized variants of RNNs such as Long Short-Term Memory (LSTM) units and Gated Recurrent Units (GRUs) that have mechanisms to mitigate these problems and handle longer sequences. These mechanisms allow the model to learn to retain or forget information as needed, making them much more effective at learning long-term dependencies. Comparing RNNs to feedforward networks, RNNs have a distinct advantage when it comes to sequential data. Feedforward networks lack the capacity to handle time-dependent data since they consider each input independently. In contrast,

RNNs can process sequential data by sharing parameters across different parts of the model. This enables them to model temporal dynamics, making them better suited for tasks like language modeling, time series forecasting, and sequence generation.

However, it's important to note that RNNs can be more complex and computationally intensive to train than feedforward networks due to their recursive nature. Furthermore, feedforward networks can often be a better choice for non-sequential data or when the computational resources are limited. In a broader sense, RNNs offer unique advantages for handling sequential data, making them a powerful tool in many machine learning applications. However, like all models, they have their strengths and weaknesses, and the choice of model should depend on the specific task at hand.

Creating RNNs in PyTorch

Creating a Recurrent Neural Network (RNN) in PyTorch is quite similar to creating a Feedforward network, with some specific differences that reflect the temporal nature of the RNN.

Below is a step-by-step process of creating a simple RNN in PyTorch:

Import the necessary libraries: As usual, you will need to import PyTorch and the torch.nn module.

```python
import torch
from torch import nn
```

Define the network architecture: To define a RNN, you also subclass nn.Module. Within your new class, you define the layers of your network in the constructor and specify how data should be passed through the network in the forward method.

The following is an example of a simple RNN:

```python
class SimpleRNN(nn.Module):
    def __init__(self, input_size, hidden_size, output_size):
        super(SimpleRNN, self).__init__()
        self.rnn = nn.RNN(input_size, hidden_size, batch_first=True)
        self.fc = nn.Linear(hidden_size, output_size)
```

```python
def forward(self, x):
    out, _ = self.rnn(x)
    out = self.fc(out[:, -1, :])
    return out
```

In this network, input_size is the number of features in the input data, hidden_size is the number of features in the hidden state, and output_size is the number of output features. The line out, _ = self.rnn(x) is where the sequence data is passed through the RNN layer. The hidden state is automatically initialized to zero by PyTorch, and it's not necessary to manually initialize it. The line out = self.fc(out[:, -1, :]) is where the last hidden state is passed through the fully connected layer to generate the output.

Instantiate the network: Creating an instance of your RNN is done in the same way as for the Feedforward network:

```python
input_size = 10  # for example
hidden_size = 20  # for example
output_size = 1  # for example
model = SimpleRNN(input_size, hidden_size, output_size)
```

Define the loss function and the optimizer: These are chosen in the same way as for the Feedforward network.

```python
criterion = nn.MSELoss()  # for example
optimizer = torch.optim.Adam(model.parameters())
```

Train the network: Training the network involves the same steps as for the Feedforward network: making predictions, calculating the loss, and updating the weights.

```python
for epoch in range(num_epochs):
    # Forward pass
    outputs = model(inputs)
    loss = criterion(outputs, labels)

    # Backward and optimize
```

```
optimizer.zero_grad()
loss.backward()
optimizer.step()
```

The key difference between creating a RNN and a Feedforward network is in the definition of the network architecture. In the RNN, we make use of nn.RNN which creates a recurrent layer that takes into account the sequential nature of the data. The RNN also needs to handle the hidden state, which represents the "memory" of the network. Unlike Feedforward networks, RNNs use previous inputs to influence current predictions, which is essential for tasks involving sequential data.

However, it's worth noting that this is a very simple RNN and doesn't take into account the issues with long-term dependencies that are common in RNNs. For a more complex model that can handle these issues, you might want to consider using a Long Short-Term Memory (LSTM) or a Gated Recurrent Unit (GRU), both of which are also available in PyTorch's nn module.

Exploring Gated Recurrent Units (GRUs)

Overview

Gated Recurrent Units (GRUs) are a type of recurrent neural network architecture that were designed to combat the vanishing gradient problem found in traditional RNNs. This problem makes it hard for RNNs to maintain and learn from long-term dependencies in a sequence. The GRU, proposed by Kyunghyun Cho et al. in 2014, is simpler than the Long Short-Term Memory (LSTM) architecture, another solution to the vanishing gradient problem, but it has shown comparable performance in certain tasks.

GRUs introduce the concept of a gating mechanism, similar to LSTMs. These mechanisms are a way to control the flow of information in the network, but GRUs use two gates, compared to the three used in LSTMs:

- Update Gate (z): This gate decides what information to throw away and what new information to add. It is a mix between the current memory and the new input.

- Reset Gate (r): This gate is used to decide how much of the past information to forget.

Both of these gates are trained to selectively filter information that passes through them, using a sigmoid activation function to output values between 0 and 1, indicating the amount of information to retain or forget. The GRU maintains a hidden state similar to the RNN, but it uses these gating units to control the updates to this hidden state. This helps to preserve information over long sequences and thus allows the model to better capture dependencies in the data.

Advantages of GRUs

The primary advantage of GRUs over standard RNNs is their ability to better handle long-term dependencies in sequence data. This makes them more effective for tasks involving sequences of data with potentially important information at many time steps in the past, like time series analysis, natural language processing, and speech recognition.

Another advantage is that GRUs are generally more efficient to train than LSTMs due to their reduced complexity, while often achieving comparable performance. This can make them a good choice when computational resources or data are limited.

To summarize, GRUs are an effective and popular type of recurrent neural network that can handle long sequences of data and are a good choice for many sequence prediction tasks. Their combination of effective performance and reduced complexity compared to other architectures makes them a popular choice in the field of deep learning.

Creating Gated Recurrent Units (GRUs)

Building a Gated Recurrent Unit (GRU) model in PyTorch follows a similar process as the one we've previously discussed for the simple RNN.

Below is a step-by-step walkthrough:

Import the necessary libraries: First, you need to import PyTorch and the torch.nn module.

```
import torch
from torch import nn
```

Define the network architecture: The architecture of a GRU model in PyTorch can be defined by subclassing the nn.Module class.

The following is an example of a simple GRU:

```
class GRUModel(nn.Module):
    def __init__(self, input_size, hidden_size, output_size, num_layers):
```

```python
        super(GRUModel, self).__init__()
        self.hidden_size = hidden_size
        self.num_layers = num_layers
        self.gru = nn.GRU(input_size, hidden_size, num_layers, batch_first=True)
        self.fc = nn.Linear(hidden_size, output_size)

    def forward(self, x):
        h0 = torch.zeros(self.num_layers, x.size(0), self.hidden_size).to(x.device)
        out, _ = self.gru(x, h0)
        out = self.fc(out[:, -1, :])
        return out
```

In this network, input_size is the number of features in the input data, hidden_size is the number of features in the hidden state, output_size is the number of output features, and num_layers is the number of layers in the GRU.

The line out, _ = self.gru(x, h0) is where the sequence data is passed through the GRU layer. The initial hidden state h0 is manually initialized to zero.

The line out = self.fc(out[:, -1, :]) is where the last hidden state is passed through the fully connected layer to generate the output.

Instantiate the network: Creating an instance of your GRU is done in the same way as for the other models:

```python
input_size = 10  # for example
hidden_size = 20  # for example
output_size = 1  # for example
num_layers = 2  # for example
model = GRUModel(input_size, hidden_size, output_size, num_layers)
```

Define the loss function and the optimizer: These are chosen in the same way as for the other networks.

```python
criterion = nn.MSELoss()  # for example
```

optimizer = torch.optim.Adam(model.parameters())

Train the network: Training the network involves the same steps as for the other networks: making predictions, calculating the loss, and updating the weights.

```
for epoch in range(num_epochs):
    # Forward pass
    outputs = model(inputs)
    loss = criterion(outputs, labels)

    # Backward and optimize
    optimizer.zero_grad()
    loss.backward()
    optimizer.step()
```

You should keep in mind that GRUs, like other RNNs, work with sequences. This indicates that the input must be a tensor in three dimensions. The dimensions of this tensor, which are batch size, sequence length, and number of features, respectively, relate to their corresponding concepts. In order to accomplish this, the batch_first=True option is utilized throughout the process of constructing the GRU layer.

Understanding Convolutional Neural Networks

Overview

Convolutional Neural Networks (CNNs) are a category of Neural Networks that have proven very effective in areas such as image recognition and classification. They were designed to mimic the connectivity pattern of neurons in the human brain and have been very successful in identifying faces, objects and traffic signs apart from powering vision in robots and self driving cars.

CNNs have their "neurons" arranged in three dimensions: width, height, and depth. The neurons in a layer are only connected to a small region of the layer before it, called a receptive field. Layers close to the input layer learn to recognize simple patterns, like lines and curves. Layers further along the network combine these simple patterns to recognize more complex patterns, like shapes, and even further, objects.

Advantages of CNNs

CNNs are especially good at analyzing visual data, hence their close connection with image and video processing. The following are the key attributes and benefits for CNNs being so appealing::

- Parameter Sharing: A feature detector (like a vertical edge detector) that's useful in one part of the image is probably useful in other parts of the image. This drastically reduces the amount of parameters in the model, making it less likely to overfit, more computationally efficient and less demanding on memory.

- Local Connectivity: In CNNs, instead of fully connecting all neurons to each other, neurons are only connected to a small subset of neurons in the next layer. This mirrors the way neurons in the human visual system are connected: neurons in the retina are only connected to a small subset of neurons in the visual cortex.

- Translation Invariance: Because of parameter sharing, the network is translation invariant, meaning it can recognize an object regardless of where in the visual field it appears. A CNN trained to recognize a cat in the right side of an image will also recognize a cat on the left side.

It's important to be informed that CNNs are not necessarily "better" than RNNs or GRUs, but they serve different purposes. While CNNs excel at spatial processing (like images), RNNs and GRUs are designed for temporal processing (like time-series data or language). The best architecture often depends on the nature and structure of the data you're working with. That said, there is overlap in their capabilities and sometimes you'll see them used together, like using a CNN to extract features from an image, which are then fed into an RNN for image captioning.

Creating Convolutional Neural Networks (CNNs)

Creating a Convolutional Neural Network (CNN) model in PyTorch involves several steps, similar to creating a GRU or any other neural network. The following is a step-by-step walkthrough:

Import the necessary libraries: First, you need to import PyTorch and the torch.nn module.

```
import torch
from torch import nn
```

Define the network architecture: The architecture of a CNN model in PyTorch can be defined by subclassing the nn.Module class.

The following is an example of a simple CNN for image classification:

```python
class CNN(nn.Module):
    def __init__(self):
        super(CNN, self).__init__()
        self.conv1 = nn.Conv2d(1, 6, 5)  # 1 input image channel, 6 output channels, 5x5 square convolution kernel
        self.pool = nn.MaxPool2d(2, 2)  # Max pooling over a (2, 2) window
        self.conv2 = nn.Conv2d(6, 16, 5)  # 6 input image channel, 16 output channels, 5x5 square convolution kernel
        self.fc1 = nn.Linear(16 * 5 * 5, 120)  # an affine operation: y = Wx + b
        self.fc2 = nn.Linear(120, 84)
        self.fc3 = nn.Linear(84, 10)

    def forward(self, x):
        x = self.pool(F.relu(self.conv1(x)))
        x = self.pool(F.relu(self.conv2(x)))
        x = x.view(-1, 16 * 5 * 5)  # reshape before passing to fully connected layer
        x = F.relu(self.fc1(x))
        x = F.relu(self.fc2(x))
        x = self.fc3(x)
        return x
```

In this network, nn.Conv2d applies convolution, nn.MaxPool2d applies max pooling, and nn.Linear applies a linear transformation to the incoming data. The non-linearity (ReLU or Rectified Linear Unit) is applied after each convolutional layer and before the final fully connected layer.

Instantiate the network: Creating an instance of your CNN is done in the same way as for the other models:

```python
model = CNN()
```

Define the loss function and the optimizer: These are chosen in the same way as for the other networks.

```
criterion = nn.CrossEntropyLoss()  # for example
optimizer = torch.optim.Adam(model.parameters())
```

Train the network: Training the network involves the same steps as for the other networks: making predictions, calculating the loss, and updating the weights.

```
for epoch in range(num_epochs):
    # Forward pass
    outputs = model(inputs)
    loss = criterion(outputs, labels)

    # Backward and optimize
    optimizer.zero_grad()
    loss.backward()
    optimizer.step()
```

Keep in mind that the input to the CNN in this scenario is a four-dimensional tensor of the shape (batch size, number of channels, height, and breadth). The preceding software makes the assumption that the input consists of grayscale images of a shape (height, width), which is why there is only one input channel. If you were working with color photos, you would require three input channels: one for red, one for green, and one for blue (also written as RGB).

Combining RNN and CNN Together

CNNs and RNNs are powerful models on their own, but when combined, they can achieve impressive results by leveraging the strengths of both model types. The resulting model is often called a Convolutional Recurrent Neural Network (CRNN). The CNN excels at extracting spatial features from data such as images, while the RNN excels at learning from sequential data, making them a great fit for time-series analysis or natural language processing. When these two models are combined, the result is a model that can effectively handle tasks that involve both spatial and temporal dependencies.

In a typical CRNN, the CNN acts as a feature extractor, transforming the input into a high-level representation. This representation is then fed into the RNN, which handles the sequential aspects of the problem. For example, in the field of computer vision, a CRNN can be used for video classification tasks. The CNN component can process individual frames to extract spatial features while the RNN can use the temporal sequence of these frames to understand the motion or changes occurring across frames.

In natural language processing, a common application of CRNNs is in image captioning. The CNN processes an image and captures its features, which the RNN then uses to generate a descriptive caption.

The following is an example of how a CRNN might look:

```python
class CRNN(nn.Module):
    def __init__(self):
        super(CRNN, self).__init__()
        self.cnn = nn.Sequential(
            nn.Conv2d(1, 16, kernel_size=3, stride=1, padding=1),
            nn.ReLU(),
            nn.MaxPool2d(kernel_size=2, stride=2),
            nn.Conv2d(16, 32, kernel_size=3, stride=1, padding=1),
            nn.ReLU(),
            nn.MaxPool2d(kernel_size=2, stride=2)
        )

        self.rnn = nn.GRU(input_size=32*7*7, hidden_size=50, num_layers=2, batch_first=True)

        self.fc = nn.Linear(50, 10)  # 10 output classes

    def forward(self, x):
        batch_size = x.size(0)
        x = self.cnn(x)
        x = x.view(batch_size, -1, 32*7*7)  # Reshape before passing to RNN
        out, _ = self.rnn(x)
        out = self.fc(out[:, -1, :])  # Output of last time step
```

```
    return out
```

In this code, a two-layer CNN is used for feature extraction from an input image. The output of the CNN is then reshaped and fed into a GRU, an RNN variant. The final linear layer produces the classification output. To sum up, a CRNN combines the spatial feature extraction capabilities of a CNN with the sequence learning capabilities of an RNN, making it a powerful model for tasks involving both spatial and temporal dependencies.

Now, we will proceed with training the CRNN model. The process of training a CRNN model is very similar to training any other neural network model in PyTorch. The following is how you can do it:

Define the loss function and the optimizer: These are chosen the same way as for the other models. For example:

```
criterion = nn.CrossEntropyLoss()
optimizer = torch.optim.Adam(model.parameters())
```

Train the network: Training the network involves running a loop over the epochs, making predictions, calculating the loss, and updating the model parameters.

```
num_epochs = 100  # example value
for epoch in range(num_epochs):
    for i, (images, labels) in enumerate(train_loader):
        # Forward pass
        outputs = model(images)
        loss = criterion(outputs, labels)

        # Backward and optimize
        optimizer.zero_grad()
        loss.backward()
        optimizer.step()

        if (i+1) % 100 == 0:
            print ('Epoch [{}/{}], Loss: {:.4f}'
```

```
                .format(epoch+1, num_epochs, loss.item()))
```

In this above code snippet, train_loader is an instance of torch.utils.data.DataLoader, which loads the training data in batches. The above program assumes that your labels are in the form suitable for nn.CrossEntropyLoss (i.e., class indices rather than one-hot encoded vectors).

Evaluate the model: After the model has been trained, you can use it to make predictions on new data. The model's performance can be evaluated by comparing its predictions to the actual labels.

```
with torch.no_grad():
    correct = 0
    total = 0
    for images, labels in test_loader:
        outputs = model(images)
        _, predicted = torch.max(outputs.data, 1)
        total += labels.size(0)
        correct += (predicted == labels).sum().item()
    print('Test Accuracy of the model on the test images: {} %'.format(100 *
correct / total))
```

In this given code, test_loader is another DataLoader instance that loads the test data.

This is a simple demonstration, and there might be additional complexities in a real-world scenario. The data might need to be preprocessed or augmented, the model might need to be regularized to prevent overfitting, the learning rate might need to be adjusted over time, etc. However, this sample program should give you a solid starting point for training CRNN models.

Need of Designing Custom Layers

Designing custom layers and networks in deep learning can offer several advantages, notably task specificity, research potential, and efficiency. Each of these aspects contributes to making the custom design approach a viable and often beneficial route in various scenarios.

Task specificity plays a pivotal role in why one might opt for custom layers and networks. The multitude of tasks that deep learning models need to address cannot all be efficiently solved using standard layers and architectures. Some tasks demand a unique approach, possibly requiring special operations or specific arrangements of layers that aren't available in off-the-shelf architectures. For instance, you might need to implement a layer with a non-standard activation function or a network that integrates different types of data in unique ways. In such cases, custom layers or networks become indispensable, enabling the creation of models that can address these specific requirements effectively.

From a research perspective, the development of new layers and architectures is a fundamental component of deep learning exploration. Researchers often propose new techniques to enhance model performance or to address specific challenges in the field. Implementing these novel ideas will often necessitate the creation of custom layers or networks. If you're probing a fresh technique or a novel architecture, it's almost a certainty that you will need to design custom elements to actualize your theoretical concepts.

Lastly, the custom approach can sometimes lead to more efficient solutions than standard alternatives. Efficiency here can refer to both computational resources and the number of parameters in the model. Custom layers or networks can be designed in a way that optimizes the usage of resources, potentially leading to quicker training times or reduced memory usage. In terms of the number of parameters, custom designs might allow for more compact models, which could be particularly beneficial in scenarios where storage space or computational capacity is limited, such as on mobile devices or embedded systems.

Design Custom Layers

To bring these custom layers or networks to life in PyTorch, one typically creates a class that inherits from nn.Module, PyTorch's base class for all neural network modules. Inside this class, the forward method is defined, which outlines the forward pass of the layer or network. This is where you detail how the input data is transformed into output data, essentially dictating the layer's or network's behavior. It's important to remember that while PyTorch automatically computes gradients to facilitate backpropagation, the forward method is where the explicit operations of your layer or network need to be specified.

We will look at a simple example of a custom layer:

```python
class MyLayer(nn.Module):
    def __init__(self):
        super(MyLayer, self).__init__()
        self.weight = nn.Parameter(torch.randn(1), requires_grad=True)
```

```python
    def forward(self, x):
        return x * self.weight
```

In the given codes, MyLayer is a custom layer that scales its input by a trainable weight. nn.Parameter is a special kind of tensor that's automatically included in the parameters list of a nn.Module. This means that PyTorch will consider this weight as a trainable parameter of the model.

Now, we will define a custom network that uses this custom layer:

```python
class MyNetwork(nn.Module):
    def __init__(self):
        super(MyNetwork, self).__init__()
        self.layer1 = MyLayer()
        self.layer2 = MyLayer()

    def forward(self, x):
        x = self.layer1(x)
        x = self.layer2(x)
        return x
```

MyNetwork is a custom network that applies MyLayer twice to its input. Notice that the layers are defined in the __init__ method and applied in the forward method.

In a broader sense, designing custom layers and networks in PyTorch is a versatile and powerful tool that lets you implement any architecture you can imagine. Whether you're applying standard techniques or inventing new ones, PyTorch's flexibility makes it an excellent choice for deep learning research and development.

Summary

Overall, this chapter delved into the capabilities of PyTorch's nn module, detailing how it can be employed for creating various types of neural networks. The first part of this chapter introduced you to the concept of feedforward networks. Feedforward networks are foundational to many other types of neural networks, with the data flowing in one direction - from input to output. They have been used in numerous applications and offer the advantage of simplicity and interpretability.

Next, we ventured into the realm of Recurrent Neural Networks (RNNs), which add a new dimension to the feedforward networks by considering the temporal sequence of data. This allows them to capture patterns over time, making them particularly useful for time series analysis, natural language processing, and more. We also looked at how to create an RNN in PyTorch, demonstrating how simple it is to define and train these networks. The chapter then introduced more advanced types of RNNs, namely GRU and CNN. Gated Recurrent Units (GRUs) improve upon the traditional RNN by mitigating the vanishing gradient problem, allowing them to capture long-term dependencies better. Convolutional Neural Networks (CNNs), on the other hand, excel in image processing tasks due to their capability to extract high-level features from input images. We walked through creating these models in PyTorch, demonstrating how straightforward it is.

The chapter culminated with a discussion on combining RNN and CNN into a single model (CRNN) and the idea of designing custom layers and networks in PyTorch. The flexibility of PyTorch allows us to create new architectures that cater specifically to the unique requirements of a given task. We learned that these custom models can be built by extending the nn.Module class and defining our custom forward pass method. All these topics aim to equip you with a well-rounded understanding of PyTorch's capabilities and potential, preparing you for a wide range of deep learning tasks.

Chapter 5. Training Neural Networks in PyTorch 2.0

Neural Network Training - Overview

Training a machine learning model involves learning the optimal set of weights that can make the best possible predictions given the data. This is achieved through a process called optimization. The training process is iterative and typically involves steps like a forward pass, a backward pass, and weight updates. We will delve into the following steps more deeply:

Forward Pass: The forward pass is the process where the input data is passed through the network to generate predictions. The neural network uses the weights (initialized randomly at the start) to calculate the output. For example, in a simple linear regression problem, the forward pass would involve calculating the predicted 'y' values using the weights and the input 'x' values.

Loss Calculation: After the forward pass, the next step is to calculate the loss. The loss function measures the disparity between the network's predictions and the actual values. It provides a numerical value representing the amount of error present in the predictions. Common loss functions include Mean Squared Error for regression problems, Cross Entropy Loss for classification problems, etc. The goal of training is to minimize this loss value.

Backward Pass (Backpropagation): The backward pass, also known as backpropagation, is where the magic of neural network training happens. The backpropagation algorithm calculates the gradient of the loss function with respect to each weight in the network by applying the chain rule. In essence, it determines how much each weight contributes to the overall error.

Weight Updates: Once we know how much each weight contributes to the error, we can adjust the weights to minimize the loss. This is typically done using an optimization algorithm. The most common optimizer is Stochastic Gradient Descent (SGD). SGD updates the weights by a small step in the direction opposite to the gradient. This helps in reducing the loss. Other popular optimizers include Adam, RMSProp, etc., which adjust the learning rate dynamically to speed up convergence.

Epochs and Batches: The entire process of forward pass, backward pass, and weight updates is done iteratively over multiple cycles known as epochs. To speed up training and make better use of computational resources, data is usually divided into smaller batches. The forward and backward passes are done on each batch rather than the entire dataset, and weights are updated after each batch.

Over the years, many improvements and variations to these steps have been introduced.

For example, advanced optimization techniques like Adam and RMSProp that adapt the learning rate during training. Regularization techniques like Dropout and Batch Normalization are also commonly used during training to prevent overfitting and help the model generalize better. In a nutshell, the training process in deep learning is an intricate dance between forward passes, calculating losses, backpropagation, and updating weights. It is a systematic and iterative method for teaching a neural network to make accurate predictions, driven by the power of optimization and the calculus of backpropagation.

PyTorch optim Module

PyTorch's optim module houses a variety of optimization algorithms that can be used to train your neural network. These algorithms are crucial because they influence the speed and quality of training. The choice of optimizer can impact how quickly the model converges, or even whether it converges at all.

All optimizer classes in PyTorch's optim module inherit from the base class torch.optim.Optimizer. This class provides base functionality, including managing the parameters to be optimized, state, and hyperparameters. Each optimizer algorithm uses these functionalities and implements the specific optimization strategy in its step() method, which performs a single optimization step (i.e., parameter update).

Using Optimizer

To use an optimizer in PyTorch, you need to first instantiate the chosen optimizer class, passing the parameters of the model to be optimized and the necessary hyperparameters (like learning rate). After calculating gradients, calling optimizer.step() updates the parameters.

For example:

```
# Define the model
model = torch.nn.Linear(10, 5)
# Define the optimizer
optimizer = torch.optim.Adam(model.parameters(), lr=0.001)

# Training step
for input, target in dataset:
    optimizer.zero_grad()
```

```
output = model(input)
loss = loss_fn(output, target)
loss.backward()
optimizer.step()
```

In the code snippet above, the model's parameters are first zeroed out using optimizer.zero_grad() to ensure that no stale gradients are used. Then, after calculating the gradients with loss.backward(), the optimizer performs the parameter update based on these gradients with optimizer.step().

Overall, PyTorch's optim module offers a wide range of optimization algorithms that help to efficiently train neural networks.

Optimization Algorithms

Optimization algorithms are crucial for training machine learning models. They are iterative methods used to improve the model's performance by adjusting the model's parameters in a way that minimizes the cost function, also known as the loss function.

The following is an overview of some of the most common optimization algorithms:

Gradient Descent: This is the most basic form of an optimization algorithm. It computes the gradient of the loss function with respect to the parameters at the current position in the parameter space, then moves in the direction of steepest descent. The size of the step is determined by the learning rate. The process is repeated until the algorithm converces to a local minimum.

Stochastic Gradient Descent (SGD): This is a variant of gradient descent, where the update to the parameters is performed after computing the loss for each instance in the training dataset, rather than the entire dataset. It introduces randomness in the optimization process and can escape shallow local minima more easily.

Mini-batch Gradient Descent: This is a compromise between batch gradient descent and stochastic gradient descent. It splits the training dataset into small subsets or "mini-batches". The model parameters are updated after computing the loss for each mini-batch. This can reduce the noise in the gradient estimation and make the training process faster.

Momentum: This is a method used to accelerate SGD. It computes an exponentially weighted average of the gradients to update the parameters, which can help the algorithm converge faster and avoid local minima.

Adagrad: This algorithm adapts the learning rate for each parameter based on the history of gradients, which makes it good for dealing with sparse data.

RMSProp: This is an improvement over Adagrad that resolves its radically diminishing learning rates. It uses a moving average of squared gradients to normalize the gradient itself.

Adam (Adaptive Moment Estimation): This is currently one of the most popular optimization algorithms. It combines ideas from Momentum and RMSProp. It computes adaptive learning rates for different parameters and keeps an exponentially decaying average of past gradients, similar to momentum.

Each of these algorithms has its own strengths and weaknesses, and the choice of optimization algorithm can significantly affect the quality of the final model. Some algorithms might be better suited to certain types of data or models, and choosing the right algorithm is an important part of the model design process. In general, Adam is often a good choice for deep learning applications, due to its balance of efficiency and ease of use.

Gradient Descent

Gradient Descent is the most basic form of optimization algorithm. It's used to minimize the cost function by iteratively moving in the direction of steepest descent, as defined by the negative of the gradient. The learning rate determines the size of these steps.

In the context of machine learning, the cost function represents the error between the model's prediction and the actual data. The aim of Gradient Descent is to tweak the model's parameters such that this error is minimized.

The algorithm can be summarized as follows:

- Compute the gradient of the cost function with respect to each parameter in the parameter set.

- In the context of neural networks, the gradients are computed using backpropagation.

- Update each parameter by subtracting the learning rate times the gradient from the current parameter value.

- Repeat the steps until the algorithm converges to a local minimum.

- The learning rate is a crucial hyperparameter. If it is too small, the model will converge slowly. If it is too large, the model may skip the minimum and may even diverge.

Using Gradient Descent

In PyTorch, gradient descent and other optimization algorithms are implemented in the torch.optim module.

The following is an example of how you can use it:

```python
# Define a simple linear model
model = torch.nn.Linear(10, 5)

# Define the loss function
loss_fn = torch.nn.MSELoss()

# Define the optimizer
optimizer = torch.optim.SGD(model.parameters(), lr=0.01)

# Example data
input = torch.randn(10,)
target = torch.randn(5,)

# Training loop
for i in range(100):
    # Compute the predicted output
    output = model(input)
    # Compute the loss
    loss = loss_fn(output, target)
    # Zero the gradients
    optimizer.zero_grad()
    # Compute the gradients
    loss.backward()
    # Update the parameters
```

```
optimizer.step()
```

In the training loop, optimizer.zero_grad() is called to zero out the gradients, because PyTorch accumulates gradients by default. loss.backward() computes the gradients, and optimizer.step() updates the model parameters based on these gradients.

Stochastic Gradient Descent

Stochastic Gradient Descent (SGD) is a variation of the Gradient Descent algorithm, where instead of performing computations on the whole dataset—which is the basis of standard (or "Batch") Gradient Descent—you calculate the gradient and update weights based on small subsets of the data, or "mini-batches".

This has a couple of key advantages:

- Computational efficiency: It can make large-scale, computationally intensive models feasible to train, as only a fraction of the data needs to be loaded into memory for each step of training.

- Frequent updates: The frequent updates can lead to faster convergence towards the minimum of the loss function.

- Noise: The noisy update process can have a regularizing effect, potentially helping the model to avoid overfitting.

However, SGD also has its drawbacks, like the potential for significant noise in the update process and difficulty in choosing an appropriate size for the mini-batches.

Using Stochastic Gradient Descent

In PyTorch, SGD is also part of the torch.optim module.

The following is an example of how you can modify the previous example to use SGD:

```
# Define a simple linear model
model = torch.nn.Linear(10, 5)


# Define the loss function
loss_fn = torch.nn.MSELoss()
```

```python
# Define the optimizer - using SGD this time
optimizer = torch.optim.SGD(model.parameters(), lr=0.01)

# Example data
input = torch.randn(100, 10)
target = torch.randn(100, 5)

# Training loop
for i in range(100):
    for j in range(input.shape[0]):
        # Compute the predicted output
        output = model(input[j])
        # Compute the loss
        loss = loss_fn(output, target[j])
        # Zero the gradients
        optimizer.zero_grad()
        # Compute the gradients
        loss.backward()
        # Update the parameters
        optimizer.step()
```

In the above demonstration, the loop over j represents looping over the mini-batches. For simplicity, we've used a batch size of 1. In practice, you would likely use a larger batch size, such as 32 or 64.

Mini-batch Gradient Descent

Mini-Batch Gradient Descent (MBGD), as the name suggests, is a trade-off between Batch Gradient Descent and Stochastic Gradient Descent. In MBGD, the dataset is divided into small mini-batches of a specific size, and each mini-batch is used to compute the gradient of the loss function.

The advantages of Mini-Batch Gradient Descent are:

- Computational Efficiency: Unlike Batch Gradient Descent, MBGD does not require the whole dataset to fit into memory, which makes it a good choice for large datasets.

- Noise Reduction: Unlike SGD, the average of the samples within a mini-batch reduces the noise in the gradient compared to SGD.

- Vectorization: Most modern computing libraries and hardware (like GPUs) can take advantage of vectorized operations, which are usually more efficient than performing a large number of smaller computations.

Using Mini-batch Gradient Descent

The following is a great walkthrough on how you could modify the previous example to use mini-batches:

```python
# Define a simple linear model
model = torch.nn.Linear(10, 5)

# Define the loss function
loss_fn = torch.nn.MSELoss()

# Define the optimizer - still using SGD
optimizer = torch.optim.SGD(model.parameters(), lr=0.01)

# Example data
input = torch.randn(100, 10)
target = torch.randn(100, 5)

# Define the batch size
batch_size = 10

# Training loop
for i in range(100):
    for j in range(0, input.shape[0], batch_size):
        # Compute the predicted output
```

```python
    output = model(input[j:j+batch_size])
    # Compute the loss
    loss = loss_fn(output, target[j:j+batch_size])
    # Zero the gradients
    optimizer.zero_grad()
    # Compute the gradients
    loss.backward()
    # Update the parameters
    optimizer.step()
```

In the above demonstration, the loop over j steps in increments of batch_size, taking a slice of the input data and the target data for each mini-batch. In practice, you would also want to shuffle the input data at the start of each epoch to ensure the model doesn't learn anything from the order of the samples.

Momentum

Momentum, a concept borrowed from physics, has been cleverly applied in the realm of optimization algorithms to accelerate the learning process. The idea behind momentum is simple: an object in motion tends to maintain its trajectory unless acted upon by an external force. This principle is applied to the optimization process in machine learning to guide the optimizer effectively, ensuring smoother and quicker convergence towards the global minimum of the loss function.

Within the context of optimization, momentum functions by carrying forward a fraction of the update vector from the previous time step to the current one. This mechanism assists the optimizer in moving along relevant directions more effectively, thereby mitigating unnecessary oscillations. The momentum term effectively serves as a memory of the previous gradients, helping to guide the optimization process by dampening rapid changes in gradient directions. Momentum can be a potent tool in optimization, especially in scenarios marked by high curvature, small but consistent gradients, or noisy gradients. High curvature can lead to rapid changes in gradient direction, causing the optimization process to oscillate wildly and potentially miss the optimum. A small but consistent gradient can lead to a slow convergence towards the optimum. Noise can introduce randomness, making it harder for the optimizer to find the optimum.

In each of these cases, momentum can help significantly. It increases the update for dimensions whose gradients point consistently in the same direction, accelerating convergence in these dimensions. At the same time, it reduces updates in dimensions where the gradients frequently change direction, helping to dampen oscillations. This dual action helps make the trajectory of the optimizer more direct and less prone to oscillations, leading to faster convergence and potentially better solutions.

Using Momentum with SGD

Adding momentum to our SGD optimizer in PyTorch is as simple as adding an extra argument when we instantiate the optimizer.

We will see how this looks in practice:

```python
# Define a simple linear model
model = torch.nn.Linear(10, 5)

# Define the loss function
loss_fn = torch.nn.MSELoss()

# Define the optimizer - SGD with momentum
optimizer = torch.optim.SGD(model.parameters(), lr=0.01, momentum=0.9)

# Example data
input = torch.randn(100, 10)
target = torch.randn(100, 5)

# Define the batch size
batch_size = 10

# Training loop
for i in range(100):
    for j in range(0, input.shape[0], batch_size):
        # Compute the predicted output
        output = model(input[j:j+batch_size])
        # Compute the loss
        loss = loss_fn(output, target[j:j+batch_size])
```

```python
# Zero the gradients
optimizer.zero_grad()
# Compute the gradients
loss.backward()
# Update the parameters
optimizer.step()
```

In the above example, momentum=0.9 indicates that the gradient from the previous step counts for 90% of the momentum, which can be viewed as a type of memory that the gradient has of previous gradients. The current gradient is then added to this 90% accumulated gradient, and the result is used to update the parameters. This concept can help SGD navigate through ravines, areas where the surface curves more steeply in one dimension than in another, which are common around local optima. In these scenarios, SGD with Momentum will oscillate across the slopes of the ravine while only making hesitant progress along the bottom towards the local optimum.

Adaptive Gradient Algorithm

Adaptive Gradient Algorithm, or Adagrad, is a notable optimization algorithm designed with the flexibility to adapt the learning rate for individual parameters. This differential adaptation is particularly beneficial for dealing with sparse data, as it can ensure the optimization process is robust even when faced with infrequently occurring features.

Adagrad operates under the principle that not all parameters have the same sensitivity towards updates. In a high-dimensional space where data is sparse and feature occurrence is uneven, some parameters might be tied to frequent features, while others might be associated with infrequent ones. Adagrad ingeniously addresses this disparity by performing smaller updates for parameters associated with frequently occurring features and larger updates for those associated with infrequent features. This individualized treatment helps enhance the model's performance, particularly in contexts involving sparse datasets.

A unique trait of Adagrad lies in its method of adjusting the learning rate. It maintains a cumulative record of all past squared gradients, using this as a scaling factor for the learning rate. The more often a feature occurs, the greater the accumulated gradient, and hence, the smaller the effective learning rate. This ensures that the parameters associated with frequent features do not wildly fluctuate, providing a stable learning process. However, this method of accumulation also presents a potential drawback. Since all past squared gradients are accumulated without any restriction, the total can become quite large over long training periods, resulting in an excessively small effective learning rate. This rapid decay of the learning rate can stall the learning process prematurely in long-running tasks, making Adagrad less suitable for some deep learning applications.

Using Adagrad Algorithm

The following is an example of using the Adagrad optimizer in PyTorch:

```python
# Define a simple linear model
model = torch.nn.Linear(10, 5)

# Define the loss function
loss_fn = torch.nn.MSELoss()

# Define the optimizer - Adagrad
optimizer = torch.optim.Adagrad(model.parameters(), lr=0.01)

# Example data
input = torch.randn(100, 10)
target = torch.randn(100, 5)

# Define the batch size
batch_size = 10

# Training loop
for i in range(100):
    for j in range(0, input.shape[0], batch_size):
        # Compute the predicted output
        output = model(input[j:j+batch_size])
        # Compute the loss
        loss = loss_fn(output, target[j:j+batch_size])
        # Zero the gradients
        optimizer.zero_grad()
        # Compute the gradients
        loss.backward()
```

```python
    # Update the parameters
    optimizer.step()
```

In the above sample program, the torch.optim.Adagrad is used to instantiate the Adagrad optimizer. Like SGD, the primary argument to the Adagrad optimizer is the set of parameters to be optimized, and it also accepts learning rate (lr) as an optional parameter.

Adaptive Moment Estimation

Adaptive Moment Estimation (Adam) is a popular optimization algorithm used in training many types of deep learning models. Adam combines elements from two other popular algorithms: AdaGrad, which handles sparse gradients, and RMSProp, which handles non-stationary (i.e., rapidly changing) objectives.

The name "Adam" is derived from "adaptive moment estimation", and the algorithm is designed to compute individual adaptive learning rates for different parameters. It calculates an exponential moving average of the gradient and the squared gradient, and the parameters beta1 and beta2 control the decay rates of these moving averages.

The main advantages of Adam include:
- Straightforward to implement.
- Computationally efficient with little memory requirements.
- Invariant to diagonal rescale of the gradients.
- Well suited for problems that are large in terms of data or parameters.
- Appropriate for non-stationary objectives.
- Works well with problems with very noisy or sparse gradients.
- Provides some regularization effects.

Now, we will look at an example of using the Adam optimizer in PyTorch:

```python
# Define a simple linear model
model = torch.nn.Linear(10, 5)


# Define the loss function
loss_fn = torch.nn.MSELoss()


# Define the optimizer - Adam
optimizer = torch.optim.Adam(model.parameters(), lr=0.001)
```

```python
# Example data
input = torch.randn(100, 10)
target = torch.randn(100, 5)

# Define the batch size
batch_size = 10

# Training loop
for i in range(100):
    for j in range(0, input.shape[0], batch_size):
        # Compute the predicted output
        output = model(input[j:j+batch_size])
        # Compute the loss
        loss = loss_fn(output, target[j:j+batch_size])
        # Zero the gradients
        optimizer.zero_grad()
        # Compute the gradients
        loss.backward()
        # Update the parameters
        optimizer.step()
```

In the above sample program, torch.optim.Adam is used to instantiate the Adam optimizer. As with previous optimizers, the main argument to the Adam optimizer is the parameters to be optimized. Additionally, Adam optimizer accepts learning rate (lr) as an optional parameter, which defaults to 0.001 if not provided.

Summary

In this chapter, we delved into understanding the training process in PyTorch, with a primary focus on the concept of forward and backward pass, weight updates, and different optimization techniques available in PyTorch's optim module. We began with an overview of the training process, which involves forwarding input data through the model (forward pass), computing the loss, and updating the model weights to minimize this loss (backward pass and weight updates). The process repeats iteratively until the model performs satisfactorily.

We then explored PyTorch's optim module, which provides implementations of commonly used optimization algorithms. This module is critical because it abstracts the complexity of the optimization techniques, thus allowing us to focus on building and training our models. We discussed the concept of optimization algorithms, which are essential for updating the parameters of a model and reducing the loss function in machine learning models. Our investigation led us to various optimization techniques starting with Gradient Descent, which is the most basic and widely used optimization algorithm. We then discussed Stochastic Gradient Descent (SGD) and Mini-batch Gradient Descent, both variations of the original Gradient Descent algorithm, that aim to make the computation more efficient and noisy, leading to more robust convergence. Momentum was another concept we introduced, which accelerates SGD by navigating along relevant directions and softens the oscillation in irrelevant directions.

Subsequently, we explored Adaptive Gradient Algorithm (Adagrad) which adapts the learning rate to each parameter, performing larger updates for infrequent parameters, and smaller updates for frequent ones. Following that, we dived into the Adaptive Moment Estimation (Adam) optimization algorithm, which is a blend of RMSprop and Stochastic Gradient Descent with momentum. It adapts the learning rate for each weight in the model, which is especially helpful when dealing with sparse gradients on noisy problems. Each of these techniques was demonstrated with code examples, showing how to implement them using PyTorch. Overall, this chapter provided a comprehensive understanding of the model training process and optimization techniques in PyTorch.

CHAPTER 6: PyTorch 2.0 Advanced

Overview

In this chapter, we delve into the advanced topic of model serialization and optimization, fundamental practices for real-world machine learning applications.

Model Serialization

Model serialization plays a vital role in the life cycle of machine learning models, enabling the conversion of the model's complete state into a savable, transferrable, and reloadable format. This comprehensive representation includes every aspect that defines the model and its current state, ensuring that the model can be revived and used exactly as it was at the time of saving.

The key elements encapsulated during serialization include the model architecture – the blueprint that defines how the model is structured, including the layers and their interconnections. This design is fundamental in describing how the model processes its inputs and produces its outputs. Another significant element preserved is the model parameters – the weights and biases that the model has learned during training. These parameters are the essence of the model's learning, defining how it makes predictions or decisions. The optimizer state, which includes details like the current learning rate and other optimizer-specific parameters (like momentum in SGD), is also saved. These parameters are crucial in enabling the continuation of the training process from where it was left off.

Finally, any other variables that are part of the model's state, such as the current epoch number or performance metrics, are also serialized. This comprehensive preservation ensures a smooth resumption of training or inference, without any loss of context or information, making model serialization an essential process in machine learning model management.

Model Optimization

Model optimization is a critical step in the deployment of machine learning models, particularly aimed at enhancing efficiency and performance during the inference phase. This process employs a variety of techniques aimed at reducing the model's size, referred to as its memory footprint, and decreasing inference time. A smaller memory footprint makes the model more manageable, allowing it to be deployed on devices with limited storage capabilities, such as mobile or embedded devices. Moreover, it facilitates quicker model loading times, contributing to efficiency.

Optimization also seeks to reduce the time taken for the model to generate predictions, i.e., inference time. Faster inference times mean quicker responses, a trait that is especially beneficial in real-time applications where speed is of the essence. This can involve quantization (reducing the numerical precision of the weights), pruning (removing redundant parameters), and knowledge distillation (transferring knowledge from a large model to a smaller one).

These techniques are essential for several reasons:

- Reduced Model Size: By optimizing a model, it becomes more compact, leading to a reduction in the storage space required. This is especially important for deploying models on edge devices, which usually have limited storage.

- Increased Speed: An optimized model can make faster predictions because it has fewer parameters to process. This leads to faster decision-making, a key criterion for real-time applications.

- Reduced Energy Consumption: Less computational power means less energy consumption, a significant factor when deploying models on mobile or other battery-powered devices.

In a nutshell, model serialization and optimization play vital roles in developing efficient and effective deep learning solutions. In the next section, we'll explore how PyTorch supports these features.

Perform Model Serialization

Serialize Models

PyTorch provides two main ways to serialize models:

1. state_dict(): This method returns an OrderedDict containing the model's parameters. We will consider a simple model:

```
import torch
import torch.nn as nn


class SimpleModel(nn.Module):
    def __init__(self):
        super(SimpleModel, self).__init__()
        self.fc = nn.Linear(10, 10)
```

```python
    def forward(self, x):
        return self.fc(x)


# Initialize the model
model = SimpleModel()


# Save model parameters
torch.save(model.state_dict(), 'simple_model.pt')
```

2. torch.save: This function allows you to save the entire model including its architecture, which can then be loaded as follows:

```python
# Save the entire model
torch.save(model, 'simple_model.pth')


# Load the model
loaded_model = torch.load('simple_model.pth')
```

Optimize Models

Now we will discuss model optimization. We'll talk about quantization, one of the optimization methods.

1. Quantization

PyTorch supports both dynamic and static quantization. The following is an example of dynamic quantization:

```python
import torchvision.models as models
import torch.quantization as quantization


# Load pretrained ResNet model
resnet_model = models.resnet18(pretrained=True)


# Specify that we will be quantizing to int8
```

resnet_model.qconfig = quantization.default_qconfig

# Apply dynamic quantization
quantized_model = quantization.quantize_dynamic(resnet_model, {nn.Linear},
dtype=torch.qint8)

In the above sample illustration, we apply dynamic quantization to a pretrained ResNet model. We specify that we will be quantizing to int8 and then apply quantization only to the nn.Linear layers.

2. Model Pruning

Model pruning involves the process of eliminating unnecessary values or weights in the model, essentially reducing the total number of learnable parameters. By removing the redundant or insignificant parameters, we can create a more efficient model that maintains a comparable level of accuracy.

We will consider an example of how to perform model pruning on a pretrained ResNet-18 model using PyTorch.

```
import torch
import torch.nn as nn
import torchvision.models as models
from torch.nn.utils import prune

# Load a pretrained model
model = models.resnet18(pretrained=True)

# Pruning a specific layer (layer4[1].conv1 in this case)
parameters_to_prune = (
    (model.layer4[1].conv1, 'weight'),
)

# Using L1Unstructured method for pruning, and removing 20% of connections
prune.global_unstructured(
```

```
    parameters_to_prune,
    pruning_method=prune.L1Unstructured,
    amount=0.2,
)

# Iterating over pruned parameters to make pruning permanent
for module, parameter_name in parameters_to_prune:
    prune.remove(module, parameter_name)
```

In the above sample program, we first load a pretrained ResNet-18 model. Then, we select a specific layer to prune (layer4[1].conv1), using the L1 Unstructured pruning method, and remove 20% of connections based on their L1 norm (a measure of magnitude). Finally, we iterate over the pruned parameters and make the pruning permanent using prune.remove.

It's important to remember that the impact of different optimization methods will vary depending on the specific model and application. The method and parameters that work best for one scenario may not be the best choice for another. Hence, it's often necessary to experiment and tune the model accordingly to achieve the best balance between efficiency and performance.

Distributed Training of Deep Learning

Distributed training refers to the practice of training a deep learning model across multiple machines, each equipped with one or more GPUs. As the size of datasets and models increases, the time required to train these models also increases. Therefore, to expedite training times, machine learning practitioners often opt for distributed training.

Methods of Distributed Training

Distributed training can happen in two main ways:

1. Data Parallelism: In data parallelism, a single model is replicated across multiple GPUs, and each GPU is given a unique batch of data to perform forward and backward passes on. The gradients from each GPU are then gathered and averaged to update the model weights. This is the most common form of distributed training and is effective when your model can fit within the GPU memory.

2. Model Parallelism: In model parallelism, different parts of the model are placed on

different GPUs. For example, if you have a deep neural network with many layers, you could put the first few layers on one GPU and the remaining layers on another GPU. Model parallelism is used when the model is too large to fit into the memory of a single GPU. This method can be a bit trickier to implement because it involves manually assigning different parts of the model to different devices.

Distributed Training in PyTorch

PyTorch supports distributed training through its torch.nn.DataParallel and torch.nn.parallel.DistributedDataParallel classes for data parallelism. torch.nn.DataParallel is a wrapper that you can place around any module to make it run in parallel across multiple GPUs in a single machine.

The following is a brief example:

```
model = MyModel()
if torch.cuda.device_count() > 1:
  model = nn.DataParallel(model)
```

For multi-machine data parallelism, PyTorch provides torch.nn.parallel.DistributedDataParallel. This is more efficient than DataParallel but requires a little more setup, including launching multiple Python processes and providing network addresses and ports for communication.

Model parallelism in PyTorch typically involves manual work, splitting your model into different parts and assigning them to different devices using .to(device).

Distributed training has the potential to greatly decrease training times by leveraging multiple GPUs, but it also increases the complexity of your training code and can lead to more difficult debugging situations. So, it's usually considered when the benefits outweigh these complexities.

Using DataParallel to Perform Distributed Training

To start with distributed training in PyTorch, you need multiple GPUs on your machine. PyTorch provides a number of utilities and classes to help with distributed training, and a common starting point is to use torch.nn.DataParallel.

The following is an example of how you could use DataParallel to train a model across multiple GPUs:

```python
# Import necessary modules
import torch
import torch.nn as nn
import torch.optim as optim

# Define your own model
class MyModel(nn.Module):
    def __init__(self):
        super(MyModel, self).__init__()
        self.linear = nn.Linear(10, 10)

    def forward(self, x):
        return self.linear(x)

# Check if multiple GPUs are available
if torch.cuda.device_count() > 1:
    print("Let's use", torch.cuda.device_count(), "GPUs!")
    model = MyModel()
    model = nn.DataParallel(model)

model.to('cuda')

# Your training code here
optimizer = optim.SGD(model.parameters(), lr=0.001)
criterion = nn.MSELoss()

for epoch in range(10):  # loop over the dataset multiple times
    for i, data in enumerate(trainloader, 0):
        # get the inputs; data is a list of [inputs, labels]
        inputs, labels = data[0].to('cuda'), data[1].to('cuda')

        # zero the parameter gradients
```

```python
optimizer.zero_grad()

# forward + backward + optimize
outputs = model(inputs)
loss = criterion(outputs, labels)
loss.backward()
optimizer.step()
```

This script will automatically use all GPUs available on the machine. The data is split in the batch dimension, so the batch size should be larger than the number of GPUs used.

However, DataParallel has its limitations, and for more complex cases, you'll likely want to move to DistributedDataParallel. This API can distribute the workload on multiple GPUs across several machines, but it is also more complex to set up.

It's also important to keep in mind that distributed training doesn't automatically mean faster training. There is a communication overhead as gradients need to be shared and synced between GPUs, so depending on your model architecture and batch size, you might not see a linear speedup.

PyTorch Quantization API

Understanding Quantization

Quantization is a technique that allows for computations to be performed at a lower precision than the original data representation. The primary motivation behind quantization is to save on memory and computational resources, enabling the deployment of large machine learning models on devices with limited resources such as mobile devices or embedded systems.

Quantization in the context of deep learning is the process of reducing the number of bits that represent the weights and activations of a neural network. It is a form of network compression that allows for a dramatic reduction in the memory footprint of a neural network, and a significant increase in the computational speed of a network, especially on hardware with fixed-point arithmetic capabilities.

PyTorch's quantization API provides implementation for both quantization aware training (QAT) and post-training quantization (PTQ). Quantization Aware Training mimics the effects of quantization during the forward pass of the network, allowing the network to learn to compensate for quantization error in the weights and activations. This leads to a much smaller accuracy drop when the network is subsequently quantized.

On the other hand, post-training quantization is a method where the model is trained using traditional methods and then the weights are quantized post training. This technique is simpler and faster but may lead to a larger drop in accuracy in comparison to QAT.

Components of PyTorch Quantization

Below are some key components of PyTorch's quantization API:

- QuantStub and DeQuantStub: PyTorch provides QuantStub and DeQuantStub to mark the points in a model where data needs to be converted from floating point to quantized representation and vice versa.

- Quantized Operators: PyTorch provides implementations for many commonly used operators in their quantized form, like convolution and linear layers, ReLU, sigmoid, etc.

- QConfig: This is an object that defines several important details about how quantization should be applied to a layer or operation. This includes the type of quantization (symmetric, asymmetric), the granularity (per-tensor, per-channel), and the scheme for quantizing weights and activations.

- torch.quantization.prepare and torch.quantization.convert: These functions handle the details of applying quantization to a model. The prepare function modifies a model in-place to make it compatible with quantization, while the convert function finalizes the quantization process by converting the weights of the model from floating point to the appropriate quantized form.

- Quantization-aware Training (QAT): PyTorch also provides support for QAT, which simulates the effect of quantization during training.

Keep in mind that quantization frequently leads in a loss of some accuracy, but this compromise could be acceptable in circumstances where having a smaller model size and operating at a greater speed are essential.

Perform Quantization for Model Compression and Efficient Inference

We will start by creating a simple model in PyTorch and we'll apply the post-training static quantization method to it:

```python
import torch
import torch.nn as nn
import torch.quantization as quantization

class SimpleModel(nn.Module):
    def __init__(self):
        super(SimpleModel, self).__init__()
        self.fc1 = nn.Linear(10, 10)
        self.relu1 = nn.ReLU()
        self.fc2 = nn.Linear(10, 2)
        self.relu2 = nn.ReLU()

    def forward(self, x):
        x = self.fc1(x)
        x = self.relu1(x)
        x = self.fc2(x)
        x = self.relu2(x)
        return x

# Create an instance of the model
model = SimpleModel()

# Set model in evaluation mode
model.eval()

# Fuse the model for better performance
model = quantization.fuse_modules(model, [['fc1', 'relu1'], ['fc2', 'relu2']])
```

```python
# Specify quantization configuration
qconfig = quantization.get_default_qconfig('fbgemm')

# Prepare the model for static quantization
model.qconfig = qconfig
quantization.prepare(model, inplace=True)

# Calibrate the model with calibration data, this step is crucial to determine
quantization parameters
# Assuming we have a DataLoader `calibration_loader` for calibration data
for data, labels in calibration_loader:
    model(data)

# Convert to quantized model
quantization.convert(model, inplace=True)
```

In this simple example, we're creating a basic neural network with two fully connected layers and applying ReLU activation function to the outputs. The model is first fused using the fuse_modules function to combine the linear and ReLU layers for each operation into a single module. This increases the efficiency of the quantized model and is a recommended step before quantization.

We then prepare the model for quantization with the prepare function. This prepares the model for quantization by inserting observers in the model that will observe the weights and activation tensors during calibration.

Next, the model is calibrated using calibration data. Calibration is crucial as it allows the observers to determine the statistics of the weights and activations, which are then used to determine appropriate quantization parameters (scale and zero point).

Finally, we convert the model to a quantized model with the convert function. This replaces the float modules with quantized counterparts and switches the weights and activations to quantized equivalents.

Summary

In this chapter, we delved into the advanced features of PyTorch 2.0, focusing on model serialization, optimization, distributed training, and the PyTorch Quantization API.

Starting with model serialization and optimization, we learned that PyTorch provides robust functionalities for saving and loading models, which is crucial for both the intermediate checkpointing and the final deployment of models. By serializing the model's state_dict, we can preserve learned parameters for later use or inference. Optimization, on the other hand, is about improving the model's speed and reducing memory consumption. Techniques like model pruning and quantization were discussed, which could drastically reduce the computational resources required by the model without significant degradation in performance. We then explored distributed training, an essential technique for training large models or dealing with massive datasets. It allows us to parallelize computation across multiple GPUs or even machines, thus speeding up the training process. PyTorch offers multiple ways to facilitate distributed training, such as data parallelism and distributed data parallelism. Practical examples were given on how to perform distributed training in PyTorch 2.0, highlighting the crucial steps to follow.

Finally, we discussed PyTorch's Quantization API, a feature that allows us to convert the weights and activation outputs from floating-point representation to a lower-bit, typically integer representation. Quantization can greatly reduce both the memory footprint of the model and the computational resources needed for inference, which is especially important for deploying models on resource-constrained devices. We learned about static quantization and how to implement it using the PyTorch API. Throughout this chapter, we continually built on the fundamental principles of PyTorch 2.0 to explore its more advanced capabilities. This knowledge is critical for developing efficient deep learning models and systems.

CHAPTER 7. MIGRATING FROM TENSORFLOW TO PYTORCH 2.0

Why PyTorch over TensorFlow?

In this chapter, we examine the comparative analysis between TensorFlow 2.0 and PyTorch 2.0, two of the most popular open-source libraries used for machine learning and deep learning projects. While both libraries provide comprehensive, flexible platforms for developing and deploying machine learning models, they have several differences in terms of design philosophy, ease of use, performance, and support for different platforms.

TensorFlow originally adopted a static computational graph paradigm, meaning that the entire computation graph had to be defined and compiled before running the model. However, with TensorFlow 2.0, eager execution was introduced, enabling operations to run immediately as they are called within Python. This change brought TensorFlow closer to PyTorch's dynamic computational graph paradigm, where computations are executed immediately. PyTorch's approach is often considered more intuitive and pythonic, providing a gentler learning curve for newcomers and more straightforward debugging.

PyTorch has generally been appreciated for its user-friendly nature. Its dynamic computation graphs offer more flexibility and are easier to debug than the original static graphs of TensorFlow. However, with TensorFlow 2.0, TensorFlow's ease of use has significantly improved with the introduction of eager execution and the simplification of its API. In terms of performance, both TensorFlow and PyTorch provide efficient implementations for a wide range of algorithms. TensorFlow has traditionally been known for its high performance and has robust support for distributed computing and production deployment, especially on Google Cloud Platform. However, PyTorch's performance has improved significantly with each new release, and it has excellent GPU acceleration and support for distributed computing.

TensorFlow excels in deployment, particularly in production environments. It supports a wide range of platforms and languages, offering TensorFlow Serving for server-based applications, TensorFlow Lite for mobile and edge devices, and TensorFlow.js for browser-based applications. PyTorch, on the other hand, has made considerable strides in deployment options with TorchServe and the TorchScript language, which allows for the export of models to be run in a non-Python environment. Both TensorFlow and PyTorch have large, active communities providing a wealth of resources, tutorials, and pre-trained models. TensorFlow, being older, has a slightly larger community and more resources available. However, PyTorch's popularity has been rapidly increasing, particularly in the research community. TensorFlow 2.0 provides seamless integration with Keras, a high-level neural network API, making it simpler to create models with TensorFlow. PyTorch integrates well with the rest of the Python ecosystem, including NumPy and various visualization libraries.

Both TensorFlow 2.0 and PyTorch 2.0 have their unique strengths and the choice between the two often depends on the specific requirements of the project, the development and deployment environment, and personal preference. Despite the differences, both libraries continue to evolve, often learning from each other, and are essential tools in the deep learning space.

Dominance of PyTorch

In the recent years, PyTorch has gained considerable popularity especially among researchers and practitioners owing to several factors:

User-Friendly Nature: PyTorch's syntax and workflow operations are more "pythonic" than TensorFlow. Its simple and intuitive API makes it easier to work with, and understand. The ease of debugging and the ability to integrate seamlessly with the rest of Python's ecosystem makes PyTorch superior in terms of user experience.

Dynamic Computation Graphs: PyTorch uses dynamic computation graphs, also known as define-by-run approach, compared to the static computation graphs, or define-and-run approach used by TensorFlow (prior to version 2.0). This allows developers to change the graph on the fly and operations can be executed immediately. This is especially useful in models where the graph changes dynamically, such as in recurrent neural networks. This provides more flexibility and makes PyTorch more suitable for experimentation and research where flexibility and speed are crucial.

Research Adoption: PyTorch has gained significant traction in the research community due to its simplicity, efficiency, and ease of use. Most new research papers, particularly in fields requiring complex models like Reinforcement Learning and Natural Language Processing, are accompanied by PyTorch implementations. The clear and explicit nature of PyTorch code makes these papers more accessible and easier to understand.

Strong Backward Compatibility: PyTorch has a more consistent API and strong backward compatibility. This reduces the overhead of learning new methods and avoids issues arising from deprecated or significantly altered functions.

Robust Ecosystem: PyTorch's ecosystem is vast, and includes powerful extensions like PyTorch Lightning and Hugging Face's Transformers. Its interoperability with other Python libraries (like NumPy) is also superior.

Superior Performance: While traditionally TensorFlow was considered to have an edge in terms of performance, PyTorch has closed the gap significantly, especially with newer versions. It provides excellent GPU acceleration and support for distributed computing.

While both PyTorch and TensorFlow have their strengths, PyTorch's flexibility, ease of use, dynamism, and robustness make it a preferred choice for many researchers and developers. However, it's important to be informed that the choice between PyTorch and TensorFlow should be determined based on the specific needs and constraints of your project. Both frameworks continue to evolve and have strong support from their communities.

Migration from TensorFlow to PyTorch 2.0

The process of moving a model from TensorFlow to PyTorch comprises a number of phases. As a straightforward illustration, let's take a look at the problem of converting a straightforward fully connected (dense) neural network that was trained using the MNIST dataset.

Understand TensorFlow Model

Before we can convert the model, we need to understand its architecture, input and output dimensions, and training configuration. A typical TensorFlow 2.0 model might look like this:

```
import tensorflow as tf
from tensorflow.keras.models import Sequential
from tensorflow.keras.layers import Dense, Flatten
from tensorflow.keras.datasets import mnist

# Load data
(x_train, y_train), (x_test, y_test) = mnist.load_data()

# Normalize the input data
x_train = x_train.astype('float32') / 255
x_test = x_test.astype('float32') / 255

# Define the model
model = Sequential([
    Flatten(input_shape=(28, 28)),
    Dense(128, activation='relu'),
```

```
    Dense(10)
])

# Compile the model
model.compile(optimizer='adam',
        loss=tf.keras.losses.SparseCategoricalCrossentropy(from_logits=True),
        metrics=['accuracy'])

# Train the model
model.fit(x_train, y_train, epochs=5)
```

Create Equivalent PyTorch Model

Next, we'll create the equivalent PyTorch model. PyTorch requires us to define the model as a class, which inherits from the nn.Module class:

```
import torch
from torch import nn
from torchvision import datasets, transforms

# Load data
train_data = datasets.MNIST(root='data', train=True, download=True,
transform=transforms.ToTensor())
test_data = datasets.MNIST(root='data', train=False, download=True,
transform=transforms.ToTensor())
train_loader = torch.utils.data.DataLoader(train_data, batch_size=64)
test_loader = torch.utils.data.DataLoader(test_data, batch_size=64)

# Define the model
class Net(nn.Module):
    def __init__(self):
        super(Net, self).__init__()
        self.flatten = nn.Flatten()
```

```python
        self.fc1 = nn.Linear(28*28, 128)
        self.fc2 = nn.Linear(128, 10)

    def forward(self, x):
        x = self.flatten(x)
        x = torch.relu(self.fc1(x))
        x = self.fc2(x)
        return x

model = Net()
```

Specify Loss Function and Optimizer

In TensorFlow, these are specified when you compile the model. In PyTorch, you specify them separately:

```python
criterion = nn.CrossEntropyLoss()
optimizer = torch.optim.Adam(model.parameters(), lr=0.001)
```

Train the Model

In TensorFlow, you call model.fit(). In PyTorch, you have to write the training loop yourself:

```python
for epoch in range(5):  # loop over the dataset multiple times
    for images, labels in train_loader:
        # zero the parameter gradients
        optimizer.zero_grad()

        # forward + backward + optimize
        outputs = model(images)
        loss = criterion(outputs, labels)
        loss.backward()
        optimizer.step()
```

It is worth noting that there are also automated tools and libraries like ONNX (Open Neural Network Exchange) that can help with migrating models between different deep learning frameworks, including TensorFlow and PyTorch. However, it's important to understand the process and potential differences between the frameworks when doing the conversion.

Successful Strategy for Complex Model Migration

Differences in the ways that TensorFlow and PyTorch handle computations, memory management, and other aspects might make it difficult to successfully migrate complicated models or custom layers from one framework to the other.

The following is the approach that has proven to be the most effective and can still be considered valid:

- Understand the architecture: Start by fully understanding the architecture of the TensorFlow model you're converting. This includes the order of layers, types of layers, and parameters used for each layer.

- Start Small: Begin by converting smaller parts of the model to ensure that each section is working as expected.

- Reuse Pretrained Models: Both TensorFlow and PyTorch have libraries of pretrained models (tf.keras.applications and torchvision.models respectively). If the model you are trying to convert is similar to one of these pretrained models, you can modify the existing one to match your architecture, which can be easier than creating from scratch.

- Custom Layers: In TensorFlow, you define custom layers by subclassing tf.keras.layers.Layer. In PyTorch, you subclass torch.nn.Module. The main difference is that in TensorFlow, you split the computation between the build method (for creating weights) and the call method (for the computation), while in PyTorch, all the computation is done in the forward method.

- Handle Data Differently: TensorFlow and PyTorch have different ways of handling and feeding data into models. TensorFlow uses tf.data.Dataset, while PyTorch uses torch.utils.data.DataLoader. Ensure you're correctly converting your data pipeline.

- Gradient Handling: PyTorch allows more explicit and fine-grained control over gradients. If your model involves complex operations like gradient clipping or manipulation, you must confirm that you understand how PyTorch handles gradients.

- Check Your Work: After you've done the initial conversion, you must check that the PyTorch model is performing as expected. This could involve comparing the output to the TensorFlow model for the same input, checking the training curve, or verifying that the model can overfit a small dataset.

- Use ONNX: ONNX (Open Neural Network Exchange) is an open format for representing machine learning models, which supports both PyTorch and TensorFlow. You can try to convert your TensorFlow model to ONNX, then from ONNX to PyTorch. However, ONNX does not support all TensorFlow operations, so this might not work for more complex models.

- Ask for Help: The PyTorch community is quite large and active, and there are plenty of resources online for getting help with specific problems. If you're stuck on a specific issue, don't hesitate to ask for help!

ONXX (Open Neural Network Exchange)

ONNX, or Open Neural Network Exchange, is a powerful, open-source, community-driven project that enables models to be interchangeable among various Artificial Intelligence (AI) frameworks. Initiated by Microsoft and Facebook in 2017, ONNX has since received backing from many companies, including IBM, Amazon, Huawei, and many more. It offers a universal format for AI models, allowing developers to use and switch among any frameworks according to their project's requirements. This versatility not only promotes efficiency but also allows for a high degree of collaboration and sharing among developers, facilitating growth in the AI community.

ONNX is built around a computation graph model. In this model, nodes represent mathematical operations, while edges represent the multi-dimensional data arrays (tensors) communicated between them. The ONNX specification defines an extensive list of operators - mathematical operations that span primitive linear algebraic and arithmetic functions, basic signal processing operations, and common functions in neural networks.

ONNX provides a robust framework for machine learning interoperability. It can export models from one framework and import them into another for inferencing. For instance, a deep learning model developed and trained in PyTorch can be exported to the ONNX format and then imported into TensorFlow for inference, or vice versa. This allows developers to choose the best framework for the task at hand, whether it be model creation, training, or inferencing.

A significant advantage of ONNX is its ability to optimize models across different frameworks. Once a model is in the ONNX format, ONNX's optimization APIs can be leveraged to fuse multiple nodes into one, remove useless nodes, or do constant folding, thereby improving computational efficiency. These shared optimizations can reduce the need for each individual framework to implement their optimization methods, leading to a reduction in redundancy and an increase in consistency.

Another key aspect of ONNX is hardware and platform independence. Since ONNX models can be deployed on various hardware and platforms, developers can implement their models on their platform of choice. This could be a local machine, cloud platforms like Azure or AWS, or even edge devices like mobiles or IoT devices. This feature greatly expands the reach of machine learning models, moving beyond high-end servers into everyday devices.

ONNX also promotes model transparency. ONNX's protobuf-based format enables the model to be represented in a human-readable format. This transparency allows developers to understand, inspect, and even modify the model if needed. Having such a high level of transparency can be invaluable during the model development and debugging stages.

The support for ONNX is continually growing. Several popular machine learning tools and libraries, including PyTorch, TensorFlow, Scikit-Learn, CoreML, CUDA, and more, support ONNX. In addition to these tools, there are several visualizers available that can provide a graphical view of ONNX models, aiding in understanding and debugging.

To sum up, ONNX is a significant step towards making machine learning models more shareable and interoperable. Its standardized format allows for models to move freely among different frameworks, enabling developers to choose the best tools and platforms according to their needs. Its shared optimization, hardware independence, and model transparency features make it a crucial tool for modern machine learning development. Whether you're a machine learning researcher or a developer, ONNX can help you streamline your workflows and broaden your model's reach.

Using ONXX to Convert TensorFlow Model

We will start with a simple example of converting a TensorFlow model to PyTorch using the ONNX format. For simplicity, we'll work with a pre-trained TensorFlow model. TensorFlow's pre-trained MobileNet model will be used for this sample demonstration. MobileNet is a lightweight model for mobile and embedded vision applications.

Installation

Before we start, we need to confirm that TensorFlow, PyTorch, ONNX, and a converter library called ONNX-TF are installed.

You can install these using pip:

```
pip install tensorflow
pip install torch torchvision
pip install onnx
pip install onnx-tf
```

Loading Pre-trained TensorFlow Model

Next, we import the necessary libraries and load the pre-trained MobileNet model.

```
import tensorflow as tf

model = tf.keras.applications.MobileNetV2(weights='imagenet',
include_top=True)
```

In the above code, tf.keras.applications.MobileNetV2 is used to load the pre-trained MobileNet model, and weights='imagenet' specifies that we want the version of the model that was trained on the ImageNet dataset.

Converting TensorFlow Model to ONNX

After loading the TensorFlow model, we convert it to ONNX using the tf2onnx converter.

First, you need to install the tf2onnx converter.

You can do this with pip:

```
pip install tf2onnx
```

Then, we convert the model:

```python
import tf2onnx

# The input signature of the TensorFlow model needs to be specified for
conversion.
input_signature = [
    tf.TensorSpec([1, 224, 224, 3], tf.float32, name='input')
]
onnx_model, _ = tf2onnx.convert.from_keras(model, input_signature)
```

In this given codes, tf2onnx.convert.from_keras is used to convert the model. The input_signature argument defines the shape and data type of the model's input tensor.

Saving ONNX Model

After converting the model to ONNX, we save it to a file:

```python
with open('mobilenet.onnx', 'wb') as f:
    f.write(onnx_model.SerializeToString())
```

Converting ONNX Model to PyTorch

Next, we use the ONNX model to create a corresponding PyTorch model.

```python
import torch
import onnx
from onnx2pytorch import ConvertModel

# Load the ONNX model
onnx_model = onnx.load('mobilenet.onnx')

# Convert the ONNX model to PyTorch
pytorch_model = ConvertModel(onnx_model)
```

In the above code, onnx.load is used to load the ONNX model from a file, and ConvertModel is used to convert the ONNX model to a PyTorch model.

Using PyTorch Model

Now we can use the PyTorch model to make predictions. We will test the model with a dummy input:

```
# Create a random tensor with the same shape as the model's input
input_tensor = torch.randn(1, 3, 224, 224)

# Use the PyTorch model to make a prediction
output_tensor = pytorch_model(input_tensor)
```

In the above code, torch.randn is used to create a random tensor, and the PyTorch model is used to make a prediction by calling it like a function and passing the input tensor.

This whole process demonstrates the ability to take a pre-trained TensorFlow model, convert it into the ONNX format, and then convert that ONNX model into a PyTorch model. It's important to remember that not all TensorFlow operations are supported by the ONNX-TF converter, so complex models might not convert cleanly. However, for many common models, this process can be a powerful tool for using TensorFlow models in a PyTorch environment.

This ability to convert models between different formats gives developers flexibility and allows them to leverage the strengths of different frameworks. It allows for more collaboration and sharing in the machine learning community, and it helps developers avoid being locked into a single framework.

Validation of Model Conversion

After converting the model from TensorFlow to PyTorch via ONNX, you may want to validate the conversion to ensure it was successful. This process usually involves performing inference on both the original TensorFlow model and the converted PyTorch model, then comparing the outputs.

Below is a simple approach to validating your converted model:

Make TensorFlow Model Prediction

First, use your TensorFlow model to make a prediction on a sample input.

```python
import numpy as np

# Create a random input tensor in TensorFlow
input_tensor = np.random.rand(1, 224, 224, 3).astype(np.float32)

# Perform inference with TensorFlow model
tf_output = model.predict(input_tensor)
```

Make PyTorch Model Prediction

Then use the same input to make a prediction with your PyTorch model.

```python
# Convert the input to a PyTorch tensor
input_tensor = torch.from_numpy(input_tensor).permute(0, 3, 1, 2)

# Perform inference with PyTorch model
pytorch_output = pytorch_model(input_tensor)
```

Compare Output:

Finally, you can compare the outputs of the two models. A simple way to do this is by calculating the Mean Squared Error (MSE) between the two outputs.

```python
# Convert the PyTorch tensor to a NumPy array
pytorch_output = pytorch_output.detach().numpy()

# Calculate the MSE between the two outputs
mse = np.mean((tf_output - pytorch_output) ** 2)


print(f"Mean Squared Error between TensorFlow and PyTorch outputs: {mse}")
```

If the MSE is close to 0, that means the TensorFlow model and the PyTorch model produce nearly identical outputs, and the conversion was successful. Please be informed that due to differences in the underlying implementations of some operations in

TensorFlow and PyTorch, it's possible the outputs may not be exactly identical, but they should be very close.

Troubleshooting & Solutions

Using ONNX for converting models between different deep learning frameworks like TensorFlow and PyTorch can sometimes lead to complications.

Below are a few common issues and their potential solutions:

Unsupported Layers or Operations

One of the most common issues is the lack of support for certain layers or operations in ONNX, or differences in how they are implemented between different frameworks. For example, TensorFlow might support a layer that PyTorch or ONNX does not, or vice versa.

Solution: If this is the case, you may need to reimplement the unsupported layers using basic operations, or find an equivalent layer in the target framework that performs the same function.

Differences in Data Formats

TensorFlow typically uses the 'NHWC' (batch, height, width, channels) data format, while PyTorch uses 'NCHW' (batch, channels, height, width). These differences can cause errors during the conversion process.

Solution: Ensure to correctly transpose your input tensors during both conversion and inference. ONNX models usually expect 'NCHW' format.

Differences in Handling Dynamic Shapes

ONNX can have trouble with models that use dynamic shapes, particularly if the dimensions of a model's input can change between different inference sessions.

Solution: You may need to implement dynamic shape handling separately for each framework. PyTorch supports dynamic shapes natively, but for ONNX, you might need to use the ONNX Reshape operation to handle dynamic shapes.

Mismatch in Results after Conversion

Even after a successful conversion, you might encounter mismatches in the inference results.

Solution: This can be due to precision differences between frameworks, differences in how certain operations are implemented, etc. Use a variety of inputs to test the model, compare intermediate layer outputs, and fine-tune the model in the target framework if needed.

Version Incompatibility

There could be discrepancies between different versions of TensorFlow, PyTorch, and ONNX, leading to conversion issues.

Solution: Ensure that all your software libraries are updated and check the ONNX version compatibility of your TensorFlow and PyTorch versions.

A very important point to note is that every model is different, so the specific issues you encounter and their solutions will depend on the complexity and structure of your model. When troubleshooting, it can be helpful to isolate individual components of the model and convert them separately to identify where issues are arising.

Summary

This chapter mainly focused on the comparison between TensorFlow 2.0 and PyTorch 2.0, the advantages of PyTorch over TensorFlow, and the conversion of a TensorFlow model to a PyTorch model using ONNX.

We first delved into the differences between TensorFlow and PyTorch, discussing each in terms of ease of use, community support, performance, and other factors. The discussion emphasized that while both frameworks have their own strengths, PyTorch often excels in terms of user-friendliness and ease of debugging, leading to its growing popularity among researchers and developers. Further, we explored the process of migrating a TensorFlow model to PyTorch 2.0. The step-by-step walkthrough revealed that this process can be straightforward for simple models but more complex models may require a strategic approach, especially when dealing with custom layers and operations.

We then discovered ONNX (Open Neural Network Exchange), an open-source project that provides a platform-independent computational graph model for interoperability among different deep learning frameworks. ONNX offers a way to convert models between various deep learning frameworks, which can help in leveraging the strengths of different frameworks. We concluded with a hands-on demonstration of converting a TensorFlow model into a PyTorch model using ONNX. Potential issues were discussed, like unsupported layers or operations, differences in data formats, handling of dynamic shapes, mismatches in results after conversion, and version incompatibility. Solutions to these issues were also suggested, giving a rounded view of the conversion process.

Overall, this chapter offered insights into the versatility of deep learning frameworks and highlighted the important considerations when transitioning between them. It served as a reminder that choosing the right tools and understanding how to navigate between them is a crucial part of a successful deep learning project.

CHAPTER 8: END-TO-END PYTORCH REGRESSION MODEL

Stages of Building PyTorch Model

Building a deep learning model in PyTorch usually involves several key steps, which we'll describe in detail below:

Problem Definition

Understanding the issue at hand and posing it as a challenge for machine learning is always the first step in any endeavor of this kind. It is necessary for you to determine what it is that you are attempting to forecast (the target variable), as well as the information that you may use to make this prediction (the input features). In addition, you will need to choose the sort of problem you are attempting to solve (binary classification, multi-class classification, regression, etc.), as this will influence the design of your network as well as the loss function that you implement.

Data Preparation

After you have determined what the issue is, the next step is to collect and organize the relevant data. Collecting data from a variety of sources, cleaning the data, dealing with missing values, standardizing numerical values, encoding categorical values, and dividing your data into a training set and a test set are all potential steps involved in this process. Your data will need to be transformed into tensors in order for PyTorch to work with it.Tensor() or other functions that are similar to it.

Model Architecture

After that, you will proceed to specify the framework of your neural network. PyTorch includes a module called torch.nn that you may use to construct your network using pre-defined layers. These layers include things like linear, convolutional, and recurrent layers, amongst others. You are able to describe the architecture of your model within a class that inherits from the torch.nn base class.Module. In this class, you are going to declare your layers in the constructor, and then in the forward() function, you are going to specify how data is going to move through these layers.

Loss Function

The loss function is a metric that determines how accurate your model is in its predictions. It is what your model works to reduce as part of the training process. PyTorch includes a number of pre-defined loss functions in the torch for its users to choose from.nn module that you are free to utilize, such as MSELoss for problems involving regression or CrossEntropyLoss for problems involving classification.

Optimizer

The optimizer is the algorithm that updates the model parameters (weights and biases) depending on the gradients of the loss function. PyTorch has a large number of pre-defined optimizers in its torch.optim module. These optimizers include SGD, Adam, RMSProp, and many more.

Training

You are now able to train your model now that you have your data, model, loss function, and optimizer prepared. In most cases, training consists of iteratively traversing the full dataset over and over again (using epochs). During each epoch, the model will calculate the loss, compute the gradients, and update the parameters. Additionally, the model will make predictions for each data point.

Evaluation

Following the completion of the training phase, you will need to assess how well your model performs on data that it has not previously seen (your test set). You will get a sense from this of how effectively your model generalizes to new data if you do this. It is essential to keep in mind that the performance of the model while it is being trained is not always indicative of how well it will perform on data it has not previously seen.

Model Saving and Loading

Once you are satisfied with the performance of your model, you will be able to save the parameters of the model to a file. Because of this, you will no longer need to retrain the model in order to generate predictions after loading these parameters later on.

Building a PyTorch model involves a combination of these steps, tailored to the specific problem you're trying to solve. Once you've mastered these basic steps, you can move on to more advanced techniques, such as handling larger datasets with data loaders, improving your model with regularization or dropout, and speeding up training with learning rate schedules or early stopping.

Understanding Dataset

Before we begin with data preparation for building a linear regression pytorch model, we will understand the dataset available from the below url:
https://raw.githubusercontent.com/kittenpub/database-repository/main/Fish_Dataset_Pytorch.csv.

This dataset contains 7 species of fish data for market sale, having seven columns detailing various attributes of fish. It includes the following fields:

Species: This is the type of fish. As a categorical variable, it could be used for tasks like classification to predict the species of a fish based on the other variables. However, for a linear regression task, we will likely focus on the numerical variables instead.

Weight: This is the weight of the fish in grams. As a numerical variable, it could serve as a target for a regression task, where we aim to predict the weight based on other measurements.

Length1: This is the vertical length of the fish in cm.

Length2: This is the diagonal length of the fish in cm.

Length3: This is the cross length of the fish in cm.

Height: This is the height of the fish in cm.

Width: This is the diagonal width of the fish in cm.

The Length1, Length2, Length3, Height, and Width columns are numerical variables that can serve as input features for a regression task, such as predicting the weight of the fish.

Loading Dataset

To load this dataset in PyTorch, we first need to download the data and load it into a DataFrame using pandas. From there, we can convert the data to tensors and create a custom Dataset.

The following is an example of how you can do this:

```python
import pandas as pd
import torch
from torch.utils.data import Dataset


# Define a custom Dataset
class FishDataset(Dataset):
    def __init__(self, dataframe):
```

```python
        self.data = torch.tensor(dataframe.values, dtype=torch.float32)

    def __len__(self):
        return len(self.data)

    def __getitem__(self, idx):
        # Separate the features (x) from the target (y)
        x = self.data[idx, 1:]  # All columns except the first (Weight)
        y = self.data[idx, 0]  # Only the first column (Weight)
        return x, y

# Load the data into a pandas DataFrame
dataframe =
pd.read_csv("https://raw.githubusercontent.com/kittenpub/database-
repository/main/Fish_Dataset_Pytorch.csv")

# Convert the species column to one-hot encoding
dataframe = pd.get_dummies(dataframe, columns=["Species"])

# Create a Dataset from the DataFrame
dataset = FishDataset(dataframe)

# Access the first item in the Dataset
x, y = dataset[0]
print(f"Features: {x}")
print(f"Target: {y}")
```

Please be informed that we convert the species column to one-hot encoding before creating the Dataset. This is because PyTorch requires categorical variables to be in numerical format. One-hot encoding is a common way to convert categorical data to numerical data.

Creating Tensors

Once you've loaded your data into a pandas DataFrame, the next step is to convert your data into PyTorch tensors, which is the data structure that PyTorch uses for computations. This process generally involves:

1. Separating the features (inputs) and the target (output): In the case of this dataset, your features would be all the length, height, and width measurements, and your target would be the weight.

2. Converting the data to tensors: PyTorch provides several ways to convert data to tensors. For example, you can use the torch.Tensor() or torch.as_tensor() functions.

3. Splitting the data into training and test sets: This is an important step to evaluate how well your model generalizes to unseen data. You can use the train_test_split() function from sklearn to do this.

The following is an example of how you can perform these steps:

```python
import pandas as pd
import torch
from sklearn.model_selection import train_test_split

# Load the data into a pandas DataFrame
dataframe =
pd.read_csv("https://raw.githubusercontent.com/kittenpub/database-repository/main/Fish_Dataset_Pytorch.csv")

# Convert the species column to one-hot encoding
dataframe = pd.get_dummies(dataframe, columns=["Species"])

# Separate the features (x) and the target (y)
x = dataframe.drop('Weight', axis=1).values
y = dataframe['Weight'].values
```

```python
# Convert the data to tensors
x = torch.as_tensor(x, dtype=torch.float32)
y = torch.as_tensor(y, dtype=torch.float32)

# Split the data into training and test sets
x_train, x_test, y_train, y_test = train_test_split(x, y, test_size=0.2,
random_state=42)

print(f"Training set size: {len(x_train)}")
print(f"Test set size: {len(x_test)}")
```

Please be informed that we use a test size of 20%, meaning that 20% of the data is set aside for testing, and the rest is used for training. The random_state parameter is used to ensure that the splits you generate are reproducible. Different random_state values will generate different splits.

Create DataLoader Instances

Now that we have prepared our data and split it into training and test sets, we need to transform our data into PyTorch's DataLoader instances. This step is necessary because DataLoader is what feeds data into the model during training.

The DataLoader is designed to be efficient and takes care of batching, shuffling, and parallel data loading. It creates an iterable over our dataset, and the core of this iterable is the batch, which is automatically managed by PyTorch.

The following is an example of how we can create DataLoader instances for our training and test sets:

```python
from torch.utils.data import TensorDataset, DataLoader

# Define batch size
batch_size = 32

# Create TensorDatasets for the training and test sets
train_dataset = TensorDataset(x_train, y_train)
```

test_dataset = TensorDataset(x_test, y_test)

# Create DataLoaders for the training and test sets
train_loader = DataLoader(train_dataset, batch_size=batch_size, shuffle=True)
test_loader = DataLoader(test_dataset, batch_size=batch_size)

In the above sample program, we set our batch size to 32, which means that our model will be trained using 32 examples at each step. The shuffle=True parameter means that our training data will be shuffled at each epoch, which helps prevent the model from learning the order of the training data and improves generalization.

Now, our data is ready to be used for training a PyTorch model. In the training loop, you can iterate over the train_loader to get batches of training data and labels.

for batch in train_loader:
    data, labels = batch
    # continue with the training process

This is the typical data preparation pipeline when you are working with PyTorch. The DataLoader takes care of the necessary heavy lifting involved in shuffling and batching our data. It can also handle more advanced scenarios and provide a lot of additional flexibility for things like working with large datasets that don't fit in memory.

Define Model Architecture

A linear regression model is one of the simplest types of neural networks and forms the basis for many more complex models. It's particularly useful for understanding the relationship between input and output variables.

In the context of neural networks, a linear regression model can be thought of as a network with just a single layer and no activation function, or equivalently a network with a single layer followed by a linear activation function.

In the case of the fish dataset, if we're trying to predict the weight of the fish (a continuous variable), a linear regression model would be appropriate.

Now, this is the best way how you might define a simple linear regression model in PyTorch:

```python
import torch.nn as nn

# Define the model
class LinearRegressionModel(nn.Module):
    def __init__(self, input_size):
        super(LinearRegressionModel, self).__init__()
        self.linear = nn.Linear(input_size, 1)

    def forward(self, x):
        return self.linear(x)

# Initialize the model
# (We use x_train.shape[1] to get the number of input features)
model = LinearRegressionModel(x_train.shape[1])
```

This code defines a new class LinearRegressionModel that extends nn.Module, which is the base class for all neural network modules in PyTorch. The forward method defines the forward pass of the model, which is how the model makes predictions.

Finally, we instantiate the model with the number of input features as an argument, which is the number of columns in the x_train tensor.

This model is ready for training, which involves repeatedly feeding it input data and adjusting the weights and biases based on the predictions it makes, as measured by the loss function.

Train the Model

In order to train our linear regression model, we need to define both a loss function and an optimizer.

For a regression task such as this one, a common choice for the loss function is the Mean Squared Error (MSE) loss. The MSE loss computes the average squared differences between the predicted and actual values, and our goal during training is to minimize this value.

As for the optimizer, we will use the Adam optimizer. Adam stands for Adaptive Moment

Estimation and it is a popular choice because it combines the benefits of two other extensions of stochastic gradient descent. Specifically, it calculates an exponential moving average of the gradient and the squared gradient, and the parameters beta1 and beta2 control the decay rates of these moving averages.

Define MSE Loss Function

The following is how you define the MSE loss function and the Adam optimizer in PyTorch:

```python
# Define the loss function and the optimizer
criterion = nn.MSELoss()
optimizer = torch.optim.Adam(model.parameters(), lr=0.001)
```

The nn.MSELoss() function creates a criterion that measures the mean squared error between each element in the input x and target y.

The torch.optim.Adam() function creates an Adam optimizer. We pass the parameters of our model to this function so the optimizer knows which tensors it should update. The learning rate lr specifies the speed at which our optimizer should update the model's parameters.

Now, we will set our model to training mode and run a forward pass to check the initial predictions.

This can be done using the following script:

```python
# Set model to training mode
model.train()

# Run a forward pass on the model to get the initial predictions
with torch.no_grad():
    initial_predictions = model(x_train)

# Print the initial predictions
print(initial_predictions)
```

The model.train() function sets the model to training mode. This doesn't make a difference for our simple linear regression model, but for models that have different behavior during training and evaluation (like dropout or batch normalization), it's important to use this.

Next, we run a forward pass on the model to get the initial predictions. We use a context manager with torch.no_grad(): to specify that we don't want to keep track of the gradients during this operation, as we don't need them for just checking the predictions.

The initial predictions will likely be far off from the actual values, as the model's parameters are initially set to random values. This is expected, and the model should improve once we start the training process.

Now, we will delve a bit deeper into the loss function and the Adam optimizer.

A loss function, in the context of machine learning and deep learning, is a method of evaluating how well an algorithm models the given data. If the predictions deviate too much from the actual results, the loss function would output a large number. Good predictions result in a small number.

In this scenario, we're using the Mean Squared Error (MSE) loss. This is a popular loss function for regression problems. It works by calculating the average squared differences between the predicted and actual values. The squaring is necessary to remove any negative signs. It also amplifies the impact of larger errors. The equation for MSE is:

$$MSE = 1/n \; \Sigma(actual - predicted)^2$$

Where Σ is a sum over all examples, n is the total number of examples, and actual - predicted represents the difference between the actual and predicted values for each example.

Adam (Adaptive Moment Estimation) is a method that computes adaptive learning rates for each parameter. It combines the perks of two other extensions of stochastic gradient descent. Namely:

- AdaGrad: Which scales down the learning rate for each parameter adaptively, so parameters with larger gradients that are updated more also have their learning rate reduced more.

- RMSProp: Which also scales down the learning rate according to the magnitude of the gradients, but unlike AdaGrad, it uses a moving average of the squared gradient, so it doesn't decrease as fast.

Adam, in particular, computes adaptive learning rates through estimations of both the first-order moments (the mean) and the second-order moments (the uncentered variance) of the gradients.

The algorithm maintains a separate learning rate for each weight in the model and adaptively adjusts them over time. This leads to good performance with less sensitivity to the initial learning rate compared to other gradient descent optimizations.

The name "Adam" comes from the method's adaptive moment estimation, and it has been empirically shown to work well in practice and compared to other adaptive learning-method algorithms.

Now that we've covered the basics of the loss function and the optimizer, we'll be in a better position to understand the training process, which involves using the optimizer to minimize the loss function.

Training Iterations

To train the model, we need to iterate over our training data in epochs. An epoch is one complete pass through the entire training data. During each epoch, we perform the following steps:

- Run a forward pass on the input data through the model to get the predictions.

- Compute the loss based on the difference between the model's predictions and the actual values.

- Run a backward pass through the model (backpropagation) to compute the gradients of the loss with respect to the model's parameters.

- Use the optimizer to adjust the model's parameters in a way that minimizes the loss.

Below is an example of a simple training loop in PyTorch. We'll use a relatively small number of epochs (e.g., 100) for demonstration purposes:

```
# Number of epochs
epochs = 100
```

```python
# Store the losses
losses = []

for epoch in range(epochs):
    # Forward pass
    y_pred = model(x_train)

    # Compute loss
    loss = criterion(y_pred, y_train)

    # Store the loss
    losses.append(loss.item())

    # Print loss every 10 epochs
    if epoch % 10 == 0:
        print(f'Epoch {epoch}, Loss: {loss.item()}')

    # Zero gradients
    optimizer.zero_grad()

    # Backward pass
    loss.backward()

    # Update weights
    optimizer.step()

print('Training complete.')
```

During each epoch, we start by running a forward pass on the x_train data through the model to get the predictions y_pred. We then compute the loss using the criterion function, which takes the predicted and actual values as input. The zero_grad() function zeroes out any old gradients from the last iteration. Then, loss.backward() computes the new gradients, and optimizer.step() updates the model's parameters using these gradients.

We store the value of the loss during each epoch in a list of losses for later analysis. We also print the loss every 10 epochs so we can see how the model is improving during training.

This is a simple training loop, but it covers the essential components of training a neural network model with PyTorch. The actual output will depend on the data and the specific initializations of the model, but you should see the loss decrease over time as the model learns to better fit the data.

Now that we have trained our model, the next step involves evaluating our model, tuning the model if required, and making predictions on new (unseen) data.

Model Evaluation

First, we will evaluate our model to see how well it has learned from the training data. To do this, we run our model on the test data. The steps include setting the model in evaluation mode, running the forward pass, and then computing the loss:

```python
# Set model to evaluation mode
model.eval()

# Forward pass on test data
with torch.no_grad():
    y_pred = model(x_test)

# Compute loss
loss = criterion(y_pred, y_test)
print(f'Test Loss: {loss.item()}')
```

In this code snippet, model.eval() tells PyTorch that we are in evaluation mode, i.e., we don't want to update any parameters. We run our model on the test data and calculate the loss. We compare this test loss with our training loss. A significant discrepancy between these two might indicate overfitting (model performs well on the training data but poorly on the unseen data).

Model Tuning

If your model isn't performing as well as you'd like, there are several parameters you might adjust to try and improve performance:

- Number of epochs: Training for more epochs might improve performance, up until a point. But be careful of overfitting.

- Learning rate: If your training loss is fluctuating wildly during training, your learning rate might be too high. If your training loss is decreasing very slowly, your learning rate might be too low.

- Model architecture: You might need a larger or more complex model to fit the data.

Finally, we can use our trained model to make predictions on new, unseen data. To do this, we simply call our model's forward function on the new data.

The following is a simple example, assuming we have some new data in x_new:

```
# Forward pass on new data
with torch.no_grad():
    y_new = model(x_new)


# Print predictions
print(y_new)
```

Do not forget that this new data should be processed in the same way as your training and test data, i.e., it should be normalized in the same way and it should be a PyTorch tensor.

With this, you have a working pipeline for training, evaluating, tuning, and making predictions with a linear regression model in PyTorch!

Save the Model

Once you are satisfied with your model's performance, you'll want to save it so you can reuse it later. In PyTorch, you typically save and load only the model parameters, not entire models, as it's more portable.

To save your model parameters, you can use torch.save:

# Save the model parameters
torch.save(model.state_dict(), 'fish_weight_model.pt')

In this code, model.state_dict() returns an OrderedDict holding the model's parameters (and gradients), and 'fish_weight_model.pt' is the file name.

Load the Model

To load your model parameters, you need to create an instance of the same model first, and then load the parameters using load_state_dict():

# Create a new model
model_new = LinearRegressionModel(input_size, output_size)

# Load the parameters from the old model
model_new.load_state_dict(torch.load('fish_weight_model.pt'))

Don't forget to call eval() method to set dropout and batch normalization layers
to evaluation mode
model_new.eval()

After these steps, model_new should have the same parameters as the model you saved. You can now perform evaluations or predictions with model_new.

Deploy the Model

Deploying the model for production involves making it available for making predictions on new data. The specifics of how you do this will depend on your production environment.

One simple way is through a web service, where your model lives on a server and makes predictions via API calls. A more complex method could be deploying the model on a distributed system for large-scale real-time predictions.

To prepare your model for deployment, you will need to ensure it is saved and can be loaded correctly. You will also need to save your data preprocessing steps (such as normalization parameters) and ensure that new data can be appropriately processed before being passed into your model.

To conclude, these are the general steps for training a neural network model in PyTorch:

- Preparing the data and converting it to tensors.
- Defining a model architecture.
- Defining a loss function and an optimizer.
- Training the model using the training data.
- Evaluating the model using test data.
- Tuning model parameters for better performance.
- Saving the model for later use.
- Deploying the model for production use.

These steps offer a general blueprint. The specifics will depend on the problem you're trying to solve, the data you have available, and the environment in which you're working. But regardless of these details, this blueprint will give you a solid foundation for working with neural networks in PyTorch.

Summary

In this chapter, we focused on building a Linear Regression model with PyTorch 2.0 to predict the weight of a fish, using a Fish Market dataset. We started by conceptualizing the necessary steps to build any PyTorch model, which include preparing the data, defining the model architecture, and setting up the training loop with a chosen loss function and optimizer. We discussed how PyTorch's design philosophy emphasizes flexibility and efficiency, allowing us to explicitly define our model architecture and manually control the training process.

We then dove into the specifics of preparing our data. We imported the Fish Market dataset and performed data normalization and conversion into PyTorch tensors, the fundamental data structure used in PyTorch. We also split the data into training and test sets, emphasizing the necessity of evaluating our model on unseen data. We underscored that these preprocessing steps are crucial for any machine learning model and PyTorch provides tools and utilities to make these steps efficient and easy to implement. Next, we discussed the Linear Regression model architecture and its implementation in PyTorch. We created a simple Linear Regression model using PyTorch's nn.Module class, explaining the significance of each component. Following the model definition, we discussed the role of the loss function and optimizer. We used the Mean Squared Error (MSE) loss function and the Adam optimizer, explaining how they work and their importance in model training. We then trained our model using a simple training loop and observed the model learning from the data, indicated by the decreasing loss value over epochs.

Lastly, we touched upon the model evaluation, tuning, and prediction phases. We explained how to evaluate a model's performance on the test set and discussed potential actions if the model's performance was not satisfactory. We also demonstrated how to make predictions on new data. Finally, we covered how to save and load a model for later use or deployment. In essence, the chapter offered a detailed walkthrough of creating a simple but complete machine learning pipeline using PyTorch 2.0. We hope that the knowledge acquired in this chapter provides a robust foundation for exploring more complex models and concepts in deep learning.

Thank You

Index

Epilogue

As we draw to a close on this in-depth investigation into PyTorch 2.0, we hope that you, our esteemed reader, have gained not only a wealth of knowledge but also an expertise in the use of this cutting-edge deep learning framework in the real world. This book was written with the intention of serving as an all-encompassing guide. It was painstakingly prepared to take you through the many levels of comprehension, beginning with the fundamentals and progressing all the way up to the most sophisticated ideas.

This voyage began with an in-depth exploration of the intriguing world of tensors, with the goal of assisting you in better appreciating the pivotal role that they play in PyTorch. Moving on, we proceeded to investigate how to design basic as well as complex PyTorch models, illuminating the concepts with real-world examples and ensuring that you are not only reading but also learning by doing as you progressed through the material.

Taking away some of the mystery surrounding the training process was a significant step in our path. This book should have successfully dissected the supposedly complicated structure of these processes by giving you a comprehensive grasp of forward pass, backward pass, and weight updates. In addition, we presented an investigation into the PyTorch optim package as well as a number of different optimization algorithms. Anyone who is interested in deep learning or works in the field should have a fundamental understanding of how the training process works and how optimization might improve results.

We delved into the more complex ideas that are at the forefront of the deep learning space, such as model serialization and optimization, distributed training, and the utilization of PyTorch's Quantization API. These ideas are at the forefront of the deep learning space. The purpose of presenting you with these ideas was to ensure that you are always up to date on the most recent tendencies and breakthroughs in your industry. We are confident that if you gain a grasp of these sophisticated concepts, it will lead to the opening of new doors for you and will drive innovation in the projects that you undertake in the future.

The contrast between TensorFlow 2.0 and PyTorch 2.0 is one of the things that sets this book apart from others in its field. We anticipated that by giving you this comparison, you would be able to make educated decisions about which framework best meets the criteria that are unique to your situation. Most notably, we presented a detailed walkthrough for transferring models created in TensorFlow to PyTorch by making use of ONNX. This guide is meant to act as a bridge between the two platforms, thereby expanding your skill set and boosting your versatility as a practitioner of deep learning.

As we come to the end of our journey, we take some time to reflect on the primary purpose of this book, which was to get you ready for a career as a network administrator. We have high hopes that this comprehensive examination of PyTorch 2.0 has helped you get one step closer to achieving your objective. You should be well on your way to making important contributions to the field of deep learning once you have finished reading this book because it will have provided you with the information and practical abilities you need.

In conclusion, we would like to extend our most sincere gratitude to you for selecting this book to serve as your guide as you investigate PyTorch 2.0. It is our genuine goal that the ideas, strategies, and insights that are presented in this book will prove to be extremely useful resources for you in your efforts to acquire more in-depth knowledge. As you finish the last page of the book, keep in mind that this represents the beginning of your fascinating trip into the wide and ever-changing world of deep learning. Continue to discover new things and educate yourself, but the most important thing is to have fun along the way!